Yes She Can

C016645650

YES SHE CAN

Why Women Own the Future

RUTH DAVIDSON

HODDER &
STOUGHTON

First published in Great Britain in 2018 by Hodder & Stoughton
An Hachette UK company

1

A CIP catalogue record for this title is available from the British Library

Hardback ISBN 9781473659223
eBook ISBN 9781473659247

Typeset in Celeste 12/18 pt by Palimpsest Book Production Limited,
Falkirk, Stirlingshire

Printed and bound in Great Britain by Clays Ltd, Elcograf S.p.A.

Hodder & Stoughton policy is to use papers that are natural,
renewable and recyclable products and made from wood grown in sustainable
forests. The logging and manufacturing processes are expected to conform to
the environmental regulations of the country of origin.

Hodder & Stoughton Ltd
Carmelite House
50 Victoria Embankment
London EC4Y 0DZ

www.hodder.co.uk

Contents

Foreword

My best friend's mum tells a story. When we were eleven and twelve, her daughter and I – always competitive – raced each other back to her house after school. As we doubled over, hands on knees and sucking in breath, she told us that John Major had just become Britain's new prime minister. I straightened up and asked, 'Can a man even *be* prime minister?'

For our entire short lives, growing up in a small village in Scotland, the most important people on the television news at night were Margaret Thatcher and the Queen. Women ruled, and there was nothing my friend and I couldn't do.

A quarter of a century on, I still believe that.

Despite a gender pay gap, lower levels of political representation, fewer women in the boardroom, a minority of films starring a female lead, a fraction of sports funding going to women, as well as men continuing to dominate the upper echelons of the military, the judiciary, the media and the clergy, the world is changing and we stand on the cusp of the first age of woman.

I believe we will look back on this time and recognise it as the point in history where the trickle became a torrent, the torrent became a flood and the flood broke the dam. Patriarchy, misogyny and sexism won't be washed away completely – human failings and petty jealousies never are – but just as you can't unboil an egg, neither can you undo the impact of a critical mass of female leaders coming to the fore at the same time. Many have had to break down barriers, overcome prejudice, put in double the work and wait twice as long for recognition, but women are now dominating and holding more ground in more areas of public life than ever before.

They are also – crucially – making it easier for those who come after. From mentoring and role-modelling programmes to gender-blind hiring practices, flexible working and gender pay audits, they feel a sense of responsibility in helping to level the playing field.

This generation of women and girls gets better grades at school than men, is more likely to enter university, makes up the majority in prestige courses, like medicine, and dominates in subjects such as law, where nearly two-thirds of newly qualified lawyers are female.

These women are there on merit alone. But, in the past, merit wasn't always enough.

That's why this book looks at those who've gone before: the pioneers who were forced to crack the glass. From world leaders to leading actresses, corporate CEOs and army special forces, each has chosen to talk of her own path in the hope it can be a signpost for others.

As well as discussing the drive, strength, talent and tenacity they've harnessed to reach the top of their chosen profession, a number have opted to talk, too, of the darker side of success.

For every punch-the-air moment, there are countless hours of doubt, fear, worry and loneliness. There are insults to be borne, prejudices to thole* and principles to be compromised. Winners have to earn it. Women have to earn it twice.

This book is for every daughter, every mother, every aunt and every niece. It tracks some of the societal shifts that have brought us to where we are, as well as featuring a few of the individuals who have helped nudge us another fraction towards the tipping point. It is not so much a handbook as a champion for the pace of change. As more and more women own the future, I hope very much that it will become an obsolete curio in my lifetime: a text to be puzzled over as to why it needed to be written at all.

In the meantime, here are the life lessons learned by some of the world's mould-breaking women, every single one showing that yes, she can.

* Scottish word meaning to suffer or endure

About This Book

This book isn't the same as most other books. There's not a narrative arc or a three-act structure with a beginning, a middle and an end. I didn't start with a story I wanted to tell, then flesh it out with characters, incidents and a neat dénouement, as you would get with a novel. It was more like there were a hundred stories I wanted to tell and a thousand voices I wanted to tell them with.

In the end, I settled on seventeen amazing women from different backgrounds – science, politics, religion, the armed forces, culture, business, sport, law, media – and asked them to set the agenda. My favourite part of being a journalist was always, always, always conducting interviews. It was asking the questions that convention and polite society stop you voicing. It was about gently leading people into revealing more than they ever thought they would so that I – and, by extension, the audience – would more fully understand. That's the bit of journalism I miss most.

Books are different from radio and television programmes, of course. There is more room to breathe and greater scope to cover more areas, from the deeply personal to the utterly professional. And this book is a mix of both.

The areas of women's empowerment I wanted to examine – from starting out and overcoming barriers to changes in women's rights around the world, to the age-old question of whether to have children and whether that affects your career – are all here, and the experiences and perspectives of my interviewees help, I believe, to see these issues in the round.

But just as these women are hugely qualified to talk on the issues examined, I wanted a bit more than that. I wanted you to feel that you weren't just getting to know their opinions, you were getting to know *them*. Even just a little. That there's a glimpse behind the curtain of their background or motivation, or an incident in their life that has stayed with them.

So, along with a wider discussion on the differences between men and women or a dissection of how far we've got to go before we see true equality, there are miniature portraits of these world-beating women in their own words. From what it's like building the richest corporation in the world and deciding to use your money for good in the poorest places, to the work that is required to make a Hollywood career look effortless. How it feels when you have to take your children into hiding because of death threats, to the euphoria of winning an Olympic medal. It's all here.

Between each chapter, there is the opportunity to understand each of these women a little better. To walk, if not a mile, then at least a few yards in their shoes.

I cannot thank my subjects enough for their honesty. I hope, as you dip into an aspect of their lives between the wider debate, you will see there is nothing inevitable about the path each has taken. They truly are remarkable.

Getting Started

I didn't grow up wanting to be a politician. When I was five, I wanted to be a sheriff with a badge, horse and gun. By eight, I wanted to be a professional snooker player. By ten, I'd decided the whip and hat of Indiana Jones meant that archaeology was for me.

Then, the night before my eleventh birthday, the Berlin Wall came down. Usually more interested in sport than politics, even I could tell this was important and worth paying attention to – confirmed when my parents let me stay up an hour later than usual to watch the late-night news bulletin.

The wave of tumult unleashed across Europe in its wake was the white noise to that part of my growing up. Individual events – the velvet revolution in Czechoslovakia, the execution of Nicolae Ceauşescu on Christmas Day – punctuated the general haze that the world might be in uproar but, according to the six o'clock news, the good guys were winning as Communism was falling.

In the era of big news, there also came the generation of big news correspondents. While America might have had the Walter Cronkites and Martha Gellhorns of old, the UK – and specifically the BBC – gave a platform to a new generation of television journalists, like John Simpson, Martin Bell and Brian Hanrahan. It also launched a fearless correspondent, unafraid to enter the eye of the storm in the Balkans, Beijing and Iraq, armed only with a microphone and a cut-glass accent.

Kate Adie became such a fixture in the UK news firmament that playground and workplace jokes started up – you knew a country was utterly f*cked the moment Kate Adie stepped off the plane.

I thought she was fabulous. I had never seen a woman so professional and unflinching amid such danger. Later, on reading her autobiography, I learned that the on-air poise masked some truly frantic scrapes. Her account of evading Chinese soldiers, being shot in the elbow, clawing her way up an eight-foot wall and flooring a policeman with a swift kick to the groin, in an effort to get footage of the Tiananmen Square massacre broadcast to the world, made her a heroine in my eyes.

When I left university, I knew what I wanted to be. I wanted to be a war correspondent.

The obvious first step was to get a job as a cub reporter with a local newspaper in my home county – *The Glenrothes Gazette* (incorporating *Leslie and Markinch News*). From there came a job as a newsreader at my local radio station, Kingdom FM, and with it, my first chance to go to a conflict zone.

In Germany for workup, practising their urban combat skills, then Kosovo on operations with the Black Watch, I met a young lieutenant from a Territorial Army regiment who was tasked with commanding regular soldiers in a theatre of war. I was immediately impressed. For someone raised on television shows like *Dad's Army*, reservists were supposed to be old, unfit and with a list of functions extending no further than the Home Guard. That you could keep your real job, train at home but serve abroad changed everything. How much better a correspondent could I be if I'd actually served?

It took a couple of job moves before I made it to the BBC – a media organisation big enough to have a reserve-forces policy that allowed me to sign up. Even better, there was a squadron of the Royal Corps of Signals housed just a few streets away from the studios.

I was army barmy. During my officer training, with a mixed cadre from all arms of the service, our intake pitched a seventeen-stone rugby-playing male police-officer-turned-infanteer against a five-foot-nothing female nurse, who barely came up to his armpit, with all sorts in between. It was brilliant.

After completing my training, I headed off to Westbury to do my pre-Sandhurst assessment during a particularly snowy February. A gung-ho attitude and cavalier disregard for personal safety resulted in a serious accident, several broken bones and an extended stay in Salisbury General Hospital.

After months of rehab, I was back in uniform – and sent almost immediately to Accident and Emergency after falling off the Pentland Hills during a night exercise. The cadre's new commanding officer declared me an 'insurance risk' to the British Army and I was medicalled out.

One thing about hospital stays and enforced changes, they give you a bit of space and distance to make decisions about what you *really* want to do. At twenty-nine, with no spouse, no kids and no mortgage, I had to choose either to stay with the BBC for ever or make a leap – before comfort, routine and responsibility restricted my freedom to decide.

At the same time, British politics was hotting up. Tony Blair had resigned and Gordon Brown had taken the short walk from 11 to 10 Downing Street.

The BBC was going through another round of redundancies and there was money on the table for anyone who wanted to walk. Increasingly frustrated with a job that required me to tell people what was going on in the country, but prevented me doing anything to change it, I decided it would be a good time to try to find a way to do my bit to serve, but out of uniform.

I submitted my application to join the Conservative Party on the same day that I requested voluntary redundancy from the BBC – 31 October 2008. The plan was to go back to university and do a master's in international development while I worked out a way to get involved.

It turned out the expenses scandal that engulfed MPs in 2009 would get there first. One casualty was the Speaker of the House of Commons, Michael Martin, who resigned, sparking a by-election in his Glasgow North East constituency. With no Territorial Army commitments, I had my evenings and weekends back and applied, successfully, to become the Conservative candidate.

Having already lost the next-door seat of Glasgow East to the SNP, Gordon Brown was reluctant to call this by-election too soon – and what I was promised would be a simple six-week campaign lasted the better part of five months. There were thirteen candidates, including the former Scottish Socialist leader and *Celebrity Big Brother* contestant Tommy Sheridan, local radio presenter and actual *Big Brother* contestant Mikey Hughes, and the baggage handler who became famous for booting the Glasgow airport bomber in the balls, John Smeaton. It was all a bit of a circus. I loved it.

I'd caught the bug. I abandoned the master's and stood again in 2010, while helping out with the central campaign from the party's press office. In 2011 I got myself elected to Holyrood in the Scottish Parliament elections. The Scottish Conservatives were not having a good 2011, losing two seats and attracting less than 12.5 per cent of the vote. The party's leader, Annabel Goldie, announced that she would stand down.

I had no intention of seeking to replace her. I was the youngest member of our parliamentary group and the only new face. I needed to learn my trade before I could even think about taking on any sort of leadership role. The party's deputy leader decided to make his pitch for the leadership based on a bold plan to revive our fortunes by divorcing the Scottish party from the UK Conservatives, changing the name and setting up as a sister grouping – a bit like the arrangement between the CDU and CSU parties in Germany. I was appalled.

I had just spent the better part of two years of my life trying to get elected in Glasgow as a Conservative – no mean feat. Now the party I had sweated for was going to wind itself up?

The idea that a new party with a new name – but essentially the same people and policies – would suddenly succeed where the current model had failed struck me as illogical. To me, we would look like Tories who were ashamed to be Tory. And I wasn't. This was the party I'd joined: it was the party I believed in, and I wanted all of our supporters and activists to be proud of it.

Growing up in a part of Scotland that had seen great industrial change, and attending a school in what was then euphemistically called an 'area with multiple indices of deprivation', I fought against the idea of the state narrowing people's horizons. Too many kids in my class had been told by one arm of government or another which house they had to live in, which school they had to go to, which jobs their parents could do and which towns they could do them in, depending on the bus routes. It was stifling, and above it all sat the pall and prejudice of low expectations.

Crucially, the 2011 Scottish election saw the return of a majority nationalist government in Scotland for the first time. There was going to be referendum on Scottish independence where a separatist first minister of Scotland would argue against a Conservative prime minister of the UK that the country should be broken up. If the deputy leader's plan succeeded – and there was no longer a Conservative party in Scotland because it had re-badged – how could David Cameron argue for Scotland to stay when his opponents could counter that even his own party wanted to leave him? It would put him – and us – in a terrible position for fighting the upcoming campaign, the most important any of us would be involved in.

After a long talk with a senior member of the Scottish party, I was persuaded to stand for the leadership. Visiting every constituency in Scotland, I met members in front rooms and hotel bars, and took part in hustings held in conference halls and even an ice rink. By the narrowest of margins and in the final round of voting, I was elected the leader of the Scottish Conservatives in November 2011. I had been a member of the party for less than three years and a politician for barely six months. I was thirty-two, most of my parliamentary group had backed other candidates and the press variously called the role I was about to undertake 'the worst job in politics' and one even went so far as to say it was 'akin to resuscitating a corpse'.

I was the youngest party leader of a major political party anywhere in the UK, as well as the least experienced. I had no idea how to lead, and on the horizon I had the single biggest and most important vote in my lifetime – on the very existence of the United Kingdom.

I might not have grown up wanting to be a politician, but through a combination of Kate Adie, the BBC's generous redundancy terms, the MPs' expenses scandal and the electoral performance of a nationalist party putting Scottish independence at the top of the UK's political agenda, I became one. And for the first time in my life I felt I was exactly where I was supposed to be, doing exactly what I was supposed to be doing.

I believe we are all the sum of what's gone before – the places we've been, the decisions we've made, the relationships we've been in and the difficulties we've overcome along the way. Politics is my second career, but I doubt it will be my last.

However, the road I took to get here has been pretty winding so far. Goodness knows where it will ultimately lead.

That's why I find stories of beginnings instructive. Just because someone works in a similar field to their parent, does that mean the choice was made for them, or did they try several other things before they came back to what they knew? Is their current career a happy tangent to something else they were pursuing? Or has tragedy diverted their course? There are so many examples of obstacles overcome and lessons to be learned from the journey rather than the destination.

Not everyone started in their chosen career as late in life as I did. And some train for the occupation that's made for them, without even knowing it. Professor Dame Sue Black is one of the pre-eminent forensic anthropologists in the world. She has spent her career solving crimes, identifying disaster victims and teaching anatomy students how to dissect dead bodies. She started her knife work at the age of twelve:

" *My parents were quite typical Scottish Presbyterian – no nonsense, a spade's a shovel. And when I was twelve my father said, 'Go and get a job because you need to earn money. Half of your income should go to your mother for board and lodging.' I thought nothing of it. My father told me to do it, so I went.*

My friend Susan had got a job in a vegetable shop on a local farm, and said, 'There's a job here if you want it.' I worked there two Saturdays and thought, I'm not doing this. This is muddy, dirty and horrible. I'd really quite like to work just across the yard in the butcher's shop.

So I got a job at the butcher's and loved it. From the minute I went in – every single Saturday, I never missed one, every single holiday, until I was seventeen – I just loved it. I learned how to make mince, how to link sausages. I used the knives. They taught me how to sharpen them, how to cut the meat, how to use the cleavers, the whole thing. Nothing ever fazed me in the butcher's shop.

Then one of her teachers showed Black the world that lay beyond her horizon.

I had the most marvellous biology teacher, Dr Archie Fraser. I would have moved planets for him, if he'd asked me. He was such a lovely man, such an inspirational teacher.

He said to me, 'You need to get some work experience.' He sent me up to Raigmore Hospital, to the medical laboratory, and I spent two afternoons there and told him, 'I'm going to be a medical laboratory technician . . .' and I remember the shock: he turned to me and swore! 'Don't be so bloody stupid, you're going to university.'

And I thought, Oh, am I? I didn't think I could. None of my family had ever been to university. I assumed I'd leave school and get a job. But because Archie said I was going to university I thought, Oh, I must be. So I applied and never told my parents.

I didn't know what I was going to do, but because Dr Fraser had said, 'You're going,' I thought it would be biology. I got into

Aberdeen University and I hated – absolutely hated – my first and second years. It was things like counting dead fruit flies with rounded bottoms and pointed bottoms – I just didn't care.

At the end of the second year you had to make a choice about junior honours and the only two things that I was any good at were histology, which is cells, and botany. And I thought, I can't name and draw plants for the rest of my life, so I'll go into anatomy.

And when they said the third year was dissection, I thought, I can do that because I've worked in a butcher's shop.

In the third year you were given a body and asked to dissect it all year – from the top of head to the tip of the toe. I named mine Henry, because we were working from Gray's Anatomy, *which was written by Henry Gray. Henry was my cadaver for the entirety of that year and I've never looked back since then.*

It's the most amazing experience to be given permission to look underneath somebody's skin and see what's in there . . . I loved the logic of it. There was no theory, this was fact.

In the fourth year, all students were expected to pick a research project, most opting for work with lab rats. Black's pathological phobia of rodents meant she begged to do anything that kept her away from furry specimens. She opted for human bone. During the course of her research, a microlight crashed along the Aberdeenshire coast. Several weeks later, a body washed up, without head, hands and feet – suspected propeller damage from a passing boat. Before the advent of DNA testing, a team from the university, including Black, was called in to help with identification of the remains. It set her future course in forensic recovery work.

I thought, I can go from the butcher's shop to the dissecting room, to the mortuary – where the body is badly decomposed – and, actually, I'm okay in this world. That was a process of desensitisation, in some ways, and meant I could work happily in that field.

Then I went to London. I applied for a job lecturing at St Thomas'. The Metropolitan Police had a case of a missing person they believed had been dismembered, body parts put into plastic bags and stuck in a landfill site.

They were bringing in bits, saying, 'Is it human or is it not?'

The pathologists were getting upset by the number of police coming in. 'Get the girl down from Anatomy,' they said.

When I got there, one policeman looked me up and down as if to say, 'Girl? What does she know?' I took the bones they'd brought, put them in a plastic bag, sealed it, stuck it on the radiator and let it warm up. I took it off the radiator, opened the bag and stuck it under his nose. 'What can you smell?'

17

'Roast lamb.'

And I said, 'Exactly. That's because it's a sheep.'

He was okay with that and thought, She's not bad.

The next bits they brought in they thought they'd have the girl down again. Gradually I won their confidence. That was when I started working with the Metropolitan Police. Before I knew it, I was at the Home Office and the Foreign Office . . .

Her progression has taken Black from war zones to disaster zones and she has worked domestically on cases of murder and sexual abuse. She fully acknowledges that it is a dark world, but believes in the importance of speaking for the dead. She also says it has been the most wonderfully fulfilling career.

I bore very easily. I'm probably hyperactive – a bit of attention deficit somewhere. I like the fact that one day you're doing something, the next day you're doing something else, and you can't predict it.

Someone might phone to say we need to be on a site that afternoon and I love not being able to plan.

I like my interaction with students because it keeps me alive mentally. I like my interaction with the police because I'm thinking, How do I solve the problem? I hate going into the courtroom – because I'm out of my comfort zone: it's always somebody else's game, with somebody else's rules. They can make you an idiot or an expert – I've been both. I just love the unpredictability of it.

I can't imagine how you prepare yourself for a day of picking through the debris after a fire trying to find remains, or how you close your eyes at night without snapshots of the horror imprinted on your eyelids. I'm not squeamish. I've had to edit raw footage of natural disasters, attend crime scenes and listen to court testimony as a journalist, but it's not the same. The warmth, care and light that Sue Black brings to her dark work are truly arresting. And while her skills were noticed way back in the butcher's shop, her empathy with victims' families and her dispassionate scientific professionalism are as much a gift as a steady hand and an encyclopaedic brain. It is a world away from the average office or, indeed, the television studio.

The BBC is the world's oldest national broadcasting organisation and the largest broadcaster in the world by headcount. Known the world over, it has reported on every major national or international news story in its near hundred-year history. In July 2015, the corporation appointed its first ever female political editor, Laura Kuenssberg. From editing her school magazine to broadcasting from 10 Downing Street, her career choices may have evolved, but her motivation has stayed broadly the same.

I grew up in a household where everyone was quite interested in the news, so having the radio on in the morning was completely standard. Having your Shreddies and hearing

Margaret Thatcher talk, my dad behind the newspaper, was normal. And on Sunday, the newspapers were always on the breakfast table.

When I was about fifteen I did work experience at a paper. I really liked it, and I got to write a piece about housing and actually put my by-line on it. But for some reason, I thought broadcasting might be better. I loved watching telly and wanted to work in it.

When I was at university I wanted to make documentaries, and I was told that a good way to get into television was to train as a journalist. So I did student radio and edited my school magazine. I'm really nosy and very interested in the world. I remember the Berlin Wall coming down – a massive event – and watching it on Newsround.

So, she started very young in journalism and broadcasting. Political journalism came much later.

I grew up in Glasgow in the eighties and early nineties – with the poll tax and such, it was a time when politics was spiky and interesting. I remember being off sick from school – which was very rare – on the day that Thatcher left Downing Street with a tear in her eye, coming out of the door, getting into the car and glancing up at the cameras.

I also grew up in a part of Glasgow where there seemed always to be interesting MPs – Roy Jenkins, Donald Dewar and then

George Galloway. So, as the boundaries moved, my mum and dad's home was always in a place where there were real characters. I suppose I was quite politically conscious, but I didn't want to be a political journalist: I wanted to make documentaries. I wanted to be the editor of Panorama. *I wanted to go and find things out, and I came to politics quite late. I thought everyone in Westminster was kind of a weirdo for being interested in Westminster.*

For Kuenssberg, television is best able to deliver the message from the corridors of power. It is precisely the accessibility of television – its ability to reach millions of homes – that appeals to her.

I'm a huge believer in the power of TV when you get it right. For all that the media has changed – and it has changed enormously since I started – people still want television.

In a rapidly evolving world it's challenging to make a traditional format feel fresh and lively, but I think the onus is on us to be creative. We have to keep pushing at the boundaries. I really love TV, and I'm trying to make TV rather than news. To make things watchable. You've got to want to watch. Otherwise, what is the point?

Laura Kuenssberg has covered every major twist and turn of UK politics in recent times: from the UK's decision to leave the European Union and the resignation of Prime Minister David Cameron, to the subsequent leadership election, installation of

Theresa May as prime minister, and snap general election in which the Conservatives lost their parliamentary majority but remained in government. So what of the path of one of Kuenssberg's more regular subjects?

Theresa May is only the second female prime minister in British political history and, at the time of writing, one of only ten female heads of government among the recognised nations of the world. She took a circuitous route into politics, studying geography, then working in finance.

I first became interested in getting into politics and becoming an MP when I was still quite a young teenager at school. I was an only child, so I got involved in quite a lot of discussions with my parents. I was brought up in an atmosphere where the news was always on and I read the paper. It wasn't always a discussion about current affairs – I used to argue with my father as to who was the best England opening batsman, things like that.

I was brought up in a vicarage, so there was that concept of public service. But I can't say there was a sort of light-bulb moment – one day when I thought, Yes, actually, that's something I would like to do. But I recognised that not everybody who wants to do it gets to do it. And that's why I pursued another career first.

Geography was the subject I enjoyed. I went to Oxford but I didn't have the idea that you had to do PPE [Politics, Philosophy and Economics – very popular among prospective MPs as it's seen as the best course for people wanting to make it into parliament]. *We were on holiday in the Lake District while I was making my decision, and on Birka Fell I looked around and thought, Geography is an interesting subject. I'm going to do that.*

I have a friend from university, who keeps telling everybody that I once said I wanted to be the first female prime minister. I honestly can't remember that. Before I went to university I did a bit of campaigning for the party – I've always been a Conservative so I didn't go through a sort of political change.

I used to go and stuff envelopes for the Conservative Association. My father didn't want me to do anything publicly because he said he was a clergyman for everybody in the parish: he didn't want anybody to think that there was anything political in it. So I just did background work behind the scenes.

After graduation, May worked for twenty years in the financial sector – including the Bank of England – and was elected as an MP at the 1997 general election. She was the first female chairman of the Conservative Party and the first woman of any political allegiance to hold two of Britain's great offices of state: she served as home secretary for more than six years before becoming prime minister.

She is not the first woman from her cohort at university to lead a country. Female world leaders may be scarce, but the then Theresa Brasier was a contemporary of former Pakistan prime minister Benazir Bhutto, to whom she owes a debt of gratitude:

It's happenstance that Benazir was at Oxford when I was there. In fact, she introduced me to my husband. It was at an Oxford University Conservative Association disco, either in late '76, or early '77. There was quite a lot of ABBA around.

Benazir had met Philip because he had been involved in a debating competition and he came up to say hello to her at the disco, and she introduced me to him.

We lost touch with her, then came back into contact at various points. It was a shock when we switched on the news after she was assassinated – it really is when you've seen somebody like that, whom you've known and has played such a part in your life.

The Very Reverend Dr Lorna Hood was just plain Lorna Mitchell when she was called to the ministry. She had grown up in the Church of Scotland, with its more than four centuries of history, but found in it few role models to follow. In fact, women had been ordained in it as ministers for less than ten years when she applied to study theology. Lorna admits to hoping secretly that she would be rejected.

My mother died when I was fifteen, and for the next four years my father was very ill. It was quite a difficult stage in my life and a difficult stage with my faith and my belief. But I always had this thing about the ministry. I remember going to my careers guidance teacher – careers guidance was then very new in schools – and saying, 'I'm thinking about being a minister.'

She just laughed and said, 'No, no. Let's be sensible,' and talked about something else.

So I thought I was going to be a teacher of history and religion, because religion was taught in those days. I went to university and did my degree in history and the principles of religion, but the ministry just would not go away. Every time I felt I was running away from it I was actually running straight into it.

I thought, The only way to sort this out is to go to selection school. But you're twenty and you look a lot younger. They'll say, 'Away you go and do something else in the meantime,' because a lot of people who were going into the ministry at that time already had careers. There were very few who were going from school or university to the ministry.

I decided to go and say, 'I want to be a minister.' I'd be turned down and could then say, 'You see, God? It wasn't me, it was them. You have to find something else for me to do.'

It's a three-day selection: you have to chair a committee, write a tactful letter and be interviewed by Church people and a psychologist. At the very first interview, on the first day, the first question was: 'Miss Mitchell, do you go out with men?'

And I said, 'Yes, I do.' I thought, I've failed already.

And the male interviewer said, 'Do you think that's right for a woman going into the ministry?'

I thought, Well, I've failed already so I might as well be honest. 'I'm not going to be a nun.'

And he said, 'Thank goodness! We get some funny women coming up here.'

I got through.

That was in the April, just a few days before my twenty-first birthday, and I started divinity at university in the September. There were about 120 men and half a dozen females. I was the youngest of the lot. There were people we knew didn't approve of women ministers, but they were very nice and I didn't have a problem with them. I didn't fight about it, I just had to be me. That was the thing, just be me. And that's how I've done in the ministry.

I switched careers after a decade doing something I thought I'd do for ever. Sue Black was unsure of her future until a mentor guided her. Laura Kuenssberg stayed in the field she'd chosen, but picked a different branch from her childhood dream. Theresa May saw a number of her contemporaries enter politics while she was still in finance, then overtook them all to become prime minister. Lorna Hood willed herself to be rejected by the profession she felt compelled to seek.

When I was a child I had a bookmark with a quotation

attributed to George Eliot: 'It is never too late to be what you might have been.' I loved the potential in that. While clearly it is not true – I will never now be an Olympic gymnast – what is clear is that there is no single route to doing what you want to do.

THERESA MAY
Prime minister, United Kingdom

Prime minister since June 2016, Theresa May was first elected to Parliament in 1997. She was the longest-serving home secretary in the modern era, a former Conservative Party chair, and founder of Women2Win, an organisation committed to encouraging and supporting more women to enter politics. She is only the second female prime minister in the UK's history.

" I know people sometimes get a bit fed up with me using this term, but I would say that, throughout my career, I've just kind of got on with things and done the best I can. That's what my parents taught me – whatever you're doing just do the best you can in that.

The first seat I was ever interviewed in was Holborn and St Pancras and the feedback I got back afterwards was that my skirt had been too short, and I'd worn a bangle that made a noise against the table when I was speaking.

I did a few selections and always came away – however disappointed I was – saying to myself, 'Was there a particular subject I didn't know enough about? Were there questions I didn't answer very well?' I'd try to analyse it and improve rather than come away and say, 'Well, it's obvious they didn't want me because I was a woman. It was unfair.' Because you don't learn that way and you don't progress that way.

When I was party chair, we put some changes through the selection process and tried to take out what I think was inadvertent bias. So the tub-thumping speech was very much the thing that tended to get people selected, but nobody tested the potential candidates' listening skills. Yes, you've got to be able to make that rousing speech, but you've also got to be able to listen to the parents at the school gate and to the constituents. So we introduced things like the interview – getting some well-known journalists to do them so that they would draw out rather more of the knowledge and understanding of the individual candidates. We changed the processes to get that better balance between the skills that were needed.

A number of us had been talking about how few female Conservative MPs there were, and it hadn't improved much. With the leadership election in 2005, we saw an opportunity to say to the candidates 'Here's what we want to do. We expect you as potential leaders of the party to pick this up and run with it.' And that was the genesis that led to Women2Win being founded.

Women2Win was the idea of that network – identifying women who might be interested, giving them the tap on the shoulder – for a lot of women, that's important. Men have this I'm-going-to-be-prime-minister-by-the-time-I'm-twenty-two back-of-the-envelope thing. Women tend to sit back a bit more and wait for somebody to say, 'Why don't you think about this?' I'm very proud of it because I think it's done a good job. It's continuing to do a good job.

I think there's a responsibility on all female MPs to show that this is a job that is not about one gender or another, it's about the skill set you have and doing the job well with those skills. I am struck by people telling me stories of their young daughters having a different attitude now because they've seen a female prime minister. I think that's important. For me, of course, there's a double whammy. As a type 1 diabetic, I'm conscious there's a message there too.

The important thing is you have to absolutely believe in what you're doing. In terms of resilience, you have to wake up every morning realising that today may not go as well as you'd hoped it would, and things are going to happen. Being home secretary for six years was quite a good preparation for that because in the Home Office I'd wake up each morning never knowing what was going to happen. **"**

VERY REVEREND DR LORNA HOOD, OBE
Minister and former moderator, General Assembly of Scotland

In the 458-year history of the Church of Scotland, Lorna Hood is the first woman parish minister to be appointed moderator of the General Assembly, the Church's foremost leader. The first woman to be ordained to word and sacrament in the Presbytery of Paisley, she has broken barriers her entire life. Appointed in 2008 as a chaplain to the Queen in Scotland, she is considered a member of the Royal Household. Lorna is a regular contributor on both radio and television and, in her retirement, has chosen to chair charities with interests as diverse as bringing youth groups together and learning the lessons of the Bosnian genocide.

❝ Very early on in my ministry I remember coming out of a baby's funeral and the minister who was waiting to go in for the next service said to me, 'You look very upset.' I said, 'I've just had a baby's funeral.' Then I got a lecture on how you had to distance yourself from these things. I said that the day I distanced myself was the day I'd leave because that's not my type of ministry. I don't think you can minister to people without being alongside them.

My son, Michael, was two when there was a vacancy in the local hospital chaplaincy team and I said I would do it, but on the condition that it was in the maternity unit. I do think

31

there are particular areas of work that, as a woman, you understand. At that time, I was the only ministerial member of the Presbytery who had been a patient in the maternity unit. I felt I had an understanding of what people had gone through.

The previous chaplain had been like an old grandpa, going round and just speaking to everyone. After the first couple of weeks I thought, How am I going to stick just going round and saying, 'What a lovely baby'? There must be more to it. Then, one day, I walked into this four-bed room, and came to the last bed and I said, 'So, another lady-in-waiting. When are you due?' She said, 'I lost my baby.' I wanted the floor to open up in a great big hole.

I went to the head of midwifery and said, 'I don't want to see people who are okay and have had a lovely baby. I want to be involved with those who have had the problems.' She said that was great because they had asked another chaplain of a different denomination to be involved in a project they had set up, and he had said no. The project was on how you deal with people who have lost their baby during pregnancy or shortly after birth. People would leave the hospital having lost a baby and had nothing.

So we were involved in developing a programme, with recommendations of how to cope with people who had had a loss. It was like opening a can of worms: the more you delved into it, the more you realised that you really hadn't dealt with it. This project was supposed to be for a couple of months and became two years.

One of the first things I did was hold a memorial service, and people came who had lost a baby forty years before. Some of the letters I got afterwards were heartbreaking: 'Thank you. This is the first time I've been able to say goodbye.' They said that they had felt guilt because they weren't allowed to talk about it. They were told to move on and have another baby.

And during that project, I discovered that my mother had had a wee boy a number of years before who had lived for just a couple of days. I don't know if my parents had any idea of where he was buried. I'm sure my mother never got over that, but it wasn't something that was discussed in the family.

So we developed things – the parents would get a handprint of the lost baby, they would maybe get a lock of hair, just all sorts of things that would help. It also gave them permission to grieve because they had had a baby. I was in the hospital during the night, called in if something had happened, and got to know a lot of people as I went through the tragedy side of life with them. Sometimes I'd be involved when babies were born with a drug addiction and would go into care because nobody wanted them – and other couples were just desperate to have a baby and it wasn't happening. Often I came out and had a big shouting match with God.

There were so many things happening in that chaplaincy as it grew and developed. I was very privileged to be part of it and to support the staff, because they went through hell as well. I was beside people at the most vulnerable times of their lives. The memorial services carried on and are still going on in the new set-up now. **"**

Overcoming Adversity

Life throws a few curveballs at everybody. I've certainly had my fair share of personal and professional tests, crises and oh-shit-what-do-I-do-now moments.

As well as the ones that feel big at the time – a company I worked for going under, finding out my (male) co-presenter at the BBC earned 40 per cent more than I did for doing exactly the same job, the break-up of a relationship I'd thought would last for ever – there are the genuinely life-changing challenges that shape your whole outlook. I've had three, two of which were physical.

When I was five, I was run over by a truck while crossing the road outside my house. It broke my leg, shattered my pelvis, crushed my main femoral artery, severed the main nerve running down the front of my right leg and inflicted internal damage. I was in hospital for a long, long time, with surgeons undertaking a life-saving operation to reconstruct the blood vessels and keep the blood flowing to my lower body, along with multiple procedures involving pins and traction to reset my leg. In hospital, my most terrifying memories are, first, of being wheeled from the ward into an entire lecture theatre of medical students so the professor could teach my case, and second (which might have induced screaming), of having a full-body cast removed. After the pins had done their job, I had been put in plaster from my armpits to my toes. The only way to get it off was to take a circular saw to it down the whole of one side of my body.

To this day my hips are off-centre, pointing one way, and one of my legs sits badly in its socket, pointing the other. I have the scars from where my ankle bones came out of the skin while I was being dragged along the tarmac, shrapnel marks from grit and stones up my right calf, and a ten-inch scar on the inside of my right thigh from where I was split from knee to crotch for the vascular reconstruction. There are three equidistant holes with scarring down the outside of my right thigh where the pins protruded from the bone, like Meccano. That's the reason I walk with such a strange, jerky-rolling motion, and why I don't wear short skirts.

The second major injury happened almost exactly twenty years later. Again, it left me in a hospital bed, miles from home, staring at the ceiling and feeling, in equal measure, sorry for and angry with myself.

When I was twenty-five, I had completed my officer training with the Territorial Army and was ready to go to Sandhurst to sit the assessments. To make sure candidates are likely to pass – and therefore won't waste everyone's time and money – a weekend of pre-assessment tests takes place at Westbury in Wiltshire. As well as assessing leadership potential, problem-solving ability, psychological suitability, communication and comprehension, there is a heavy dose of physical testing, including command tasks, an assault course – and the physical-courage test. This requires the candidate to jump head first through an open window frame on command. To pass, you have to run up, take off from a line several feet before the obstacle, and throw yourself with enough force to land beyond a line marked on the sand on the other side. My assessment took place in February after some overnight snow and I volunteered to be first up on the test (idiot), not knowing that no one had broken up the sand. It was like landing on concrete. I couldn't get up and couldn't work out why not.

Turned out, I'd broken my back. I was dispatched to Salisbury General Hospital, where I stayed for quite some time. I was discharged only after the orthotics department had built me a metal and plastic contraption that was to be my permanent waking home for the next three months.

The back brace was hateful. Uncomfortable and cumbersome, it didn't actually stop my back hurting. As anyone with chronic pain will tell you, the sheer grind of being unable to escape from the dull, throbbing ache has a really negative impact on your enthusiasm for life. Standing, sitting, lying or walking, there was no relief.

I hate being idle and, after a week at home, I decided that daytime TV would rot my brain quicker than heroin, so the only option was to go back to work. Immediately.

I badgered my GP into writing me a consent form – promising

I wouldn't drive, wouldn't undertake any activities that would require me to stand for long periods and would knock it on the head if the pain got worse. Brandishing the letter, I left the surgery and took a cab straight to the BBC to argue my boss into submission. They had a duty of care, but if my doctor acknowledged that coming back to work three months early was beneficial to my holistic health, surely they could rota me on the radio bulletins desk so I was office-bound for a bit. Although a local gas explosion a couple of weeks later meant all hands had to be on deck – with me standing at the scene for eight hours conducting interviews, which resulted in pain so bad I couldn't sleep for two nights – I still maintain it was the right thing to do. Months stuck in the house would have tested my sanity to the limit.

Both incidents have something in common. Vulnerability comes with physical frailty. You become scared for yourself, and I hate being scared.

But there is also the chance to get your head down and push through. I've never let anyone tell me I can't do something. If they do, it makes me want to prove them wrong. I'm cussed and determined and obstinate and dogged in pursuit of making things happen when all logic dictates against it. I wonder if I would still be like this if I hadn't spent a huge part of my early childhood determined to keep up with – and, in some cases, beat – my peers. From being the only child at my primary with a Zimmer frame and teased for my scars, by primary seven I played for the school netball team and the boys' football team, one of only two girls to do so.

Breaking my back taught me other lessons. The first, some

very odd men look at you in a back brace and think, There's a woman – but with handles! During the months I had to wear it, I had a number of friends' birthday parties to attend. Not one to let the small matter of broken bones stop me, I would go along to the pub or nightclub, dressed to impress but with an enormous white and silver medical device clamped over the top. Some genuine weirdos chatted me up because of it. I can only imagine what niche websites would show on a trawl of their internet history.

The second lesson was that, sometimes, you have to adapt to overcome. You can't just do everything in the same way you always did and expect the same result. Some injuries have to be managed, which requires forethought on how to work around a task rather than bulldoze a way through it. I still suffer discomfort, on average a couple of days a week, but I refuse to slow down and I'm still able to get things done. It's about picking your battles. That counts in your personal and professional life: while the direct approach can work, it isn't always the right way to get the outcome you need.

The third big intervention wasn't physical at all. It was mental.

I went to university at seventeen years old. The first generation of my family to go on to higher education, on a full grant, and coming from my local state comprehensive, I was not prepared for how lost I became. The Edinburgh University I attended in the 1990s seemed populated by incredibly confident, loud and forceful students in their twenties who had all gone to posh private schools in the Home Counties. They all knew each other, had completed A levels, instead of Scottish

Highers, and had done a gap year building orphanages in Tanzania or looking after orang-utans in Borneo. They all seemed to have money, cars, and an unshakeable belief in themselves and their own place in the world.

If I'd known then that knowledge was not the same as intelligence, and confidence no substitute for ability, I might not have struggled so much. But another event crashed into my world. A boy from my home village committed suicide. I knew him, but not well. I didn't even go to his funeral. But he had lived across the road from me for at least a decade, and we had one other thing in common. He was mown down by a driver who came off the road and mounted the pavement on the same stretch of street as I'd been hit.

His injuries had been less life-threatening than mine, but he'd required skin grafts and had had to cut the back out of his trainers for years to accommodate the damage to his heel. I'm not a psychologist, and I don't know why his death affected me as much as it did (he wasn't the first person I knew to die) but I went into a total tailspin.

I don't know whether it was long-suppressed survivor guilt or something else that was triggered in me, but I really struggled with the idea that I deserved to live – having nearly lost my life – when others with much less damaging injuries were gone. I started hurting myself: punching walls, cutting my stomach and arms with blades or broken glass, drinking far, far too much and becoming belligerent and angry, pushing people away. I was punishing myself and hating myself for it at the same time.

At eighteen, I was diagnosed with clinical depression and

put on antidepressants. I was frightened, confused and worried that I might be going mad – that this was what a mental breakdown was. After starting medication, I had desperate, dark, terrible dreams that were so vivid I couldn't tell what was real. I became anxious and paranoid. I started having suicidal thoughts. I would sometimes find myself almost outside my body, mocking myself for saying stupid things in a conversation or situation. Every time I went back to the university health centre with a fresh set of injuries, the doctor on duty just doubled my dose and things got worse. In the end, I was on the maximum dosage allowed and became so scared of sleep that, in my second year, I spent a whole term living nocturnally. I stayed up through the night and only went to bed once my flatmates had left for lectures. As an arts student with very little structured time – we were in charge of our own required reading and making sure essays were handed in – nobody much noticed or cared if classes were missed.

People categorise depression in different ways – Churchill famously called it the black dog that followed him around. For me it wasn't something behind me, there when I turned to look. It was like a smothering black blanket over my head, cutting out the sky. It was heavy, constricting, suffocating. It took away hope and energy and life.

I had mocked the leaflets I was given on the diagnosis – NHS instructions to do light activity, like housework or clearing out my cupboards. But eventually I made a decision to will myself better, and figured there must be something in all the advice on the internet. I resolved to build a structure to my days and weeks, to set short- and medium-term goals, to engage in purposeful activity that had a measurable outcome, to take regular exercise, moderate my drinking, go back to church and be kinder to myself. Most importantly to me, I threw away my pills and promised myself that, whatever happened, no matter if I slipped back, I would never take them again. I couldn't go back to a place where I didn't know what was real and what wasn't, where my emotions were hollowed out but my anxieties heightened.

After graduation, I moved back to my childhood home, got a job on the bottom rung of the local newspaper and started building myself up. I hadn't been trained in journalism – I couldn't touch-type or do shorthand – but I was smart, interested in the world around me, and loved asking people questions. If I couldn't be the best qualified, I could damn well make sure I was the hardest working. I still have a copy of every single issue of the paper that features my by-line. Later, I switched to broadcasting, getting the job as newsreader at my local radio station, graduating to bigger employers and setting myself the goal of working for the BBC by the time I was twenty-five.

The week before my twenty-fourth birthday, I was walking down the main shopping street in Glasgow when I got a call from the Corporation offering me a job. When I hung up I ducked into a side alley, jumped up and down and punched the air.

Intellectually, I know that drug therapy helps millions of people round the world and that in a different time, or with a GP who knew me, instead of the revolving door of a university health centre, I could have received treatment that helped me get better, instead of making things worse: the manufacturer of the drug I was on has since paid out millions following class-action lawsuits after evidence of increased suicidal behaviour in adolescents. More than twenty years later, the ways in which we understand and respond to mental-health issues are unrecognisable from what they once were. The stigma is much reduced, and depression is something that far more people feel able to talk about. There's a long way to go, but it helps when more people in more fields open up – when sports stars, royalty and business leaders say publicly that they have a condition they manage, and can demonstrate that it doesn't stop them achieving.

I am still frightened of going back to the place I once inhabited. When I have periods of heightened anxiety, or I can feel the weight of the black blanket start to descend, I go back to what I know works for me: structure, exercise, forward momentum, measurable outcomes.

Sometimes that's hard in a job that's a hundred miles an hour with every day different. I worried, when I was running for the party leadership, that I might not be able to do the job. That the overwhelming pressure of being a neophyte who had to make all their mistakes in public, without the support of half of my colleagues and against an old bruiser like the first minister, Alex Salmond, when the future of my country was at stake in the Scottish independence referendum, might be too much and break me. The confidence I gained from coming out of that campaign – one which mattered so much more to me than simple party politicking – not just intact, but with a greater self-knowledge about my mental strength, resilience, capacity for work and belief in my own judgement, has made me a better politician and tougher opponent. In the mental scorecard I keep, I had tested myself and passed. I know myself now.

There is a sense that that those who reach the top – particularly those who gain enough public acclaim in a certain field to become famous – have an easy life. Partly, this is cultivated on their behalf – filmmakers want to ensure the stars selling their movies look magical on the red carpet or are expensively styled for photoshoots in glossy magazines. But partly it is self-cultivated: people naturally want to show their best face to the world, so their social-media profiles show their triumphs, not the failures that can prompt crying in the night.

When someone comes to the public's attention for the first time, it is usually because they've *already* achieved something of note – they may have taken over a FTSE 500 company or won a high-profile award. The notion that they are richer, smarter, more exotic or happier than mere mortals therefore arrives fully formed. Not for them the worries and troubles of the rest of us. World-beaters are so special they must be fed on sunshine and shit rainbows, right?

And yet, and yet. Even a cursory look across the biographies of a handful of high-achieving women will reveal the same personal tragedies, doubts, losses or trauma found elsewhere. Like the rest of the population, it is how they respond to these challenges that determines future achievements.

Gemma Fay is the most capped footballer – male or female – in the UK, winning over 200 caps for Scotland. For context,

David Beckham amassed 115 appearances for England: Fay earned another eighty-eight caps on top of Beckham's record – one shy of Michael Owen's entire England career. If it takes a huge amount of application and effort to become the best in your country at a chosen sport, it takes something superhuman to remain the best for more than twenty years. Yet Fay has never had the strut of unshakeable belief that people expect of an elite athlete.

❝ *I was quite awkward growing up. I was bullied through school, mostly because of my background: we were a single-parent family. Perth is quite middle class, and everybody knows everybody. It was difficult at times. I loved sport but found it really hard to make friends. So, going to university was a fresh start for me but I still didn't have a lot of confidence.*

I've played in goal for Scotland, for the senior team, since I was sixteen. I was making the mistakes that everybody makes when they're learning to be an athlete, but I was making them on an international stage in front of cameras, in front of press. If you're not that confident a person, still trying to deal with things that happened in childhood, and all of a sudden you're thrust forward and told, 'You're not good enough, but you're all we've got', which happened, you're not going to have amazing confidence. I didn't for a long time. I'm not even sure I've got it now, but I know how to fake it.

Eventually, I figured out my own way of being a goalkeeper to the best I could be. But while I was still growing, still learning, I

45

had up-times and down-times. I probably had more down-times, but the up-times are so euphoric that they kind of feed you through the rest.

Fay combined her international duties with full-time work in sports development. Now retired, and with the benefit of distance, she uses her experience of self-doubt to help others. She teaches people that you don't have to be full of belief to push yourself and to achieve. Doubts and worries don't have to be conquered or banished for you to get past them and succeed.

I didn't really believe in myself. I believed that I was good – you don't play for Scotland if you're not good – and I believed that once I was named in the team and on the pitch I had this swagger, this arrogance, about me, this presence. But it's deep down. I didn't have this unbelievable confidence within myself. I don't think that's uncommon in sportspeople.

But there's always a perception and there's always a reality. The older I get, the more I understand that, when you tell the truth, people know it. When you put on a front, no matter how good you are, people know it.

In the work I've done mentoring athletes or with kids – I've made the best connections with them when I've told them a story which isn't about sport but about me as a human. That it's okay to be like this or that – and it's okay for certain things to happen in your life. None of it defines you as a person so don't let it.

In 2004 at the age of thirty-one, the dot-com millionaire Martha Lane Fox was severely injured in a car accident in Morocco. Her body was broken. Dozens of operations later, she still suffers chronic pain. While it has impacted on how she approaches activity and work, she has continued to break new ground.

> *I broke twenty-eight bones. I had a stroke. I smashed my pelvis in nine places. I spent two years in hospital. Now it's about managing the logistics – am I going to fall over? Am I going to have some kind of horrible accident? Am I in pain? It is all these things that you don't want your head to be focused on.*

Despite the day-to-day difficulties her injuries have created, the now Baroness Lane Fox chairs the digital-skills charity, Go ON UK, and sits or has sat on the boards of Marks & Spencer, Channel 4 and Twitter. She was elevated to the House of Lords as its youngest ever female member and has recently been appointed to the UK's Joint Committee on the National Security Strategy.

> *I get angry that I can't do all the things I want to do because I haven't quite got the capacity. That's the thing I have to manage in my head. And I think, It doesn't matter. Pick up a book, read a poem. It doesn't matter, just do your best. Those are the things that are actually harder in a way than the physical bits.*

> *Incontinence is way worse than pain. That's my huge challenge and not something people can easily see, thank God.*

I feel as if I am looking in on my body rather than actually in it, which is boring, takes up time and brain space, and absolutely affects my core identity of who I am. I don't talk about it very much. It's survival through denial. I can't go there every day in my head because it would be too overwhelming, so instead I just carry on. I know that sounds ridiculous but, literally, I just carry on.

As well as teaching, a large part of Professor Dame Sue Black's forensic career has been devoted to helping police and international authorities conduct investigations. In conversation, her commitment to victims is clear. She believes her science can speak for those who cannot speak for themselves. Her appreciation of the law, and of justice, is almost palpable.

I have a history of child abuse. I have never told anybody publicly that the reason I am an intransigent son of a bitch is simply because I won't let anybody win and I won't let anybody take control over who I am. I'm not ashamed about it, I don't hide from it, I've just never been asked the question that has allowed it to be told.

This was somebody who was known to the family, as is often the way. So as a result, you can't tell your parents because it's somebody who is a friend of theirs. My grandmother knew – she was the one who said 'You know, you're not drawn. Nobody draws you from their own eyes, you draw yourself from your own eyes, so don't listen to what other people want to make of you. You need to make of yourself what is right for you.

Look in the mirror, and if what's looking back is something you're content with, you're on the right track. Somebody else draws a picture that isn't you? That's their problem. It isn't yours.'

That made me quite determined, quite brutally determined, that I would do what I felt was right, even though there were difficulties along the way.

You choose either to survive or you become a victim. And so, through my grandmother, I chose that I was going to survive.

Professor Black's experience has had a direct impact on her professional life. She and her colleagues have adapted and developed the science around the identification of hands from the unique pattern of blood vessels beneath the skin. This has helped build cases against those accused of abusing children when imagery, such as photographs or videos of the indecent acts, exists.

In the work I do on paedophiles, it's about ensuring that the right people are on the right side of the bars, because I can't think of anything worse for a man who is accused of child sexual abuse, who is innocent, because you never get away from it. People always say 'No smoke without fire'. I am just as passionate about ensuring people are not wrongly accused, as I am that abusers get their just deserts. That is, in part, why the work that I do now is associated with indecent images of children. It's about justice and ensuring justice, and I've worked on both sides. I've worked on the prosecution, I've worked on the defence and I've been able to say to police, 'This is not your guy. I don't know who is, but it's definitely not your guy,' and that's really important.

As for me, I will never name individuals, I will never prosecute. It was a time past and that person's family don't need to carry that. So I'm still protecting people in that regard but I refuse to be a victim, absolutely refuse to be a victim, and I think – although I would never wish it to happen to anybody – I do think part of who I am is embedded within that.

You shouldn't have to find strength out of an indecent act, absolutely shouldn't, but you take your strength where you find it. And that is what my grandmother taught me.

I love the strength of women. I love that their strength stretches to the emotional honesty to tell their own story, unvarnished. I love that women – particularly those who have had hard experiences – can determine not to become hard themselves. Rather, that they want to use their experiences to help other women.

PROFESSOR DAME SUE BLACK
Professor of anatomy and forensic anthropology

Professor Sue Black is one of the country's pre-eminent forensic scientists. She has combined teaching with disaster response, body identification and criminal investigation. Her work has taken her to conflict zones in Kosovo, Iraq and areas devastated by the Indian Ocean earthquake and tsunami in 2004. At home, her work has helped to smash one of the UK's largest paedophile rings. She has spent ten years heading up the Centre for Anatomy and Human Identification at the University of Dundee, and recently took up the role of pro vice chancellor for engagement at Lancaster University. Despite the grimness of her work, she remains funny, warm and incredibly good company.

" My father never told me I was a girl, so I've never felt I had something to answer for in terms of being a girl. My father expected me to be able to cook a rhubarb crumble with my mother, but also to be able to help him French-polish a dining-table. So, growing up, I never thought, I'm in a man's world or a woman's world, because it was just me. That was a really incredible thing for a man of his generation to do.

I don't feel I have to prove myself. I'll bend the rules a bit sometimes, but that's fine as long as it gets the job done, as long as nobody feels demeaned. That's the most important thing, for me. I've never had a problem working in a man's world – which often the military and the police were – because there were different ways to do things.

For example, when we were in Kosovo, we had a French military commander and he was a very testosterone-laden man. Our team leader was an equally testosterone-laden man. Those two were never going to get on with each other, even to the point that they wouldn't communicate. So I arrived on scene and the French officer approached our lead. He went to shake hands and our lead said, 'Pfft. No,' and refused to shake his hand. I thought, Why would you do that? We need to work together. The Frenchman came up to me and put out his hand and I said, 'No, I'm sorry,' and you could see him think, Oh, God, another one, and I added, 'You're French – I thought you kissed a lady on both cheeks!' His face just lit up and I got a kiss on both cheeks, and from that point onwards he would deal with me, but not with our officer. That was his problem. There are ways in which we can get around things that might not be appropriate, might not be politically correct, but if it gets the job done, I'm okay with it.

I was the only woman on the team in Kosovo and I found that I could play the mother card really well – these people were away from home, away from their families, but I could listen to them. The most disruptive thing you could have in a team was an available woman, because then you had all sorts of other problems, but if you had a mother figure, it unquestionably gave a stability to the team dynamic that no other grouping had. So we would sit at night with a beer, and they'd

cry or rant or whatever, and then I'd say, 'You've had enough –
off to bed,' and off they'd go.

I loved the soldiers in Kosovo. I really loved them. They knew
what my fear was and they didn't take it as a girly thing. They
knew I was scared of rats and they could see it was an absolute phobia.

Where there were mass graves, they used to bury a horse or a
cow on top, so if you dug down you'd think the smell was a
dead animal and wouldn't go any further to get to the bodies.
When we were at a grave at a meat market, scraping the soil
away, there was an obvious commotion. I moved forward, to
see what was going on, and a soldier shouted my name,
looked me in the eye and said, 'Stay.'

Okay, I thought. I'm going to do exactly what I'm told. And
they had hit a rats' nest. When all the rats had gone, they said,
'Right, get in the hole.' And so I got into the hole with the
liquid horse to get to the bodies.

They never saw me as a girl. It's about finding the balance
between people who want to look after you, but not demean
you, and also recognise you've got the strength to do your
job. **"**

GEMMA FAY
The UK's most capped footballer

No football player, male or female, has represented one of the UK's home nations on more occasions than goalkeeper Gemma Fay. After making her debut aged sixteen, she was an integral part of the game's development in Scotland and a fixture in the international set-up for more than two decades. She ended her career on a high, captaining the squad at UEFA Women's Euro 2017 – the first time Scotland's women's team qualified for a major international tournament. Now retired, she works as the head of women and girls' rugby at the Scottish Rugby Union.

" Every summer I used to go to America to do football summer camps for six weeks. I would do the coaching and then I would train, so I always came back really fit for the season. I came out of uni and I started applying for jobs.

I couldn't even get past an automated interview with Standard Life in Edinburgh because I had too many qualifications. I couldn't get a job for love nor money. It was one of these 'Can you press the number of standard grades you have?' and I had eight. 'Thank you for your interview.' That was it. I ended up working in the Kingsway Tesco in Dundee. Then I applied for a job as girls' and women's football development officer because my degree is in applied sport science. I was offered the job and accepted, but I had to pass my driving test.

That was my first full-time job, and while I was there, I was signed for Leeds so I used to travel down to Leeds every weekend, play, then get the train back. I think in those days if we won we got a thirty-pound bonus, fifteen or ten if we drew, and nothing if we lost. We lost a few games.

That was the choice. I didn't realise I had any other. Maybe that was partly me not having confidence in myself, or maybe the opportunities didn't exist. Now it's very different: being a female footballer is a viable option, a career path. It is something you can do.

But there's a bigger question around girls and their engagement with physical activity. How do we connect with them, to stop them falling through the gaps? What strategies do we use to keep them engaged – boys too?

With Xboxes and video games so popular, we've got a real problem in getting kids and keeping them active. I'm concerned about it and talk about it at great length. Folk get fed up of me talking about how people consume sport but it *is* a consumer product.

People want to consume things in short, sharp bites. You see the rise of CrossFit, HIIT. It's millennial – 'I want it, and I want it now, and if you're not going to give it to me I'm going to get it from someone else.' It's whether or not sport, in its purest sense, can keep up with that, can adapt to it. Cricket is a classic example. How many versions of cricket are there now?

Things evolve rapidly and then everything else catches up. Vaping evolved rapidly. It's the same with sport. Sport evolves rapidly. You saw the Winter Olympics. I don't know half of those new events, but they're really popular. **"**

Role Models and Mentoring

I never really believed in the power of role models. Not until I reached my thirties.

I'm the sort of person that if I'm told I can't do something, I try twice as hard. Growing up, I never knew anyone in broadcasting or politics. Nobody from my village had ever gone there first. I do remember, when I was twelve or thirteen, the school invited a couple of MPs in for a Q and A session, but they just seemed like any other old white men in crumpled pinstripes. They were so unenthusiastic – a world away from us, a bunch of teenagers who'd never made any decisions and still had every option open to us. We were potential. They were tired. Why would we want to be like them?

The people I wanted to be – or, at least, wanted to measure myself against – were the people around me. My big sister, for starters.

Rae is three and a half years older than me. She's an NHS consultant cardiologist who has already given our parents four grandchildren. She is smarter, thinner, prettier and better qualified than I am or ever will be. She beat me at everything growing up, probably because I chose only to do the things she had been doing for years. She rode horses? I wanted lessons. She played the clarinet? I wanted to do the same. She started the high-school debating team? Well, I'd make a floor speech during the interval at her competitions, with all the wisdom a squeaky-voiced primary-school kid could muster.

When she left for university, I was fourteen and started spending more time on the things I already enjoyed, separate to her. Good at ball sports, I got the first of my coaching badges in squash and tennis. I played squash at junior county level and, later, for my university. I set up a theatre company at school with the help of the English department and we put on an adaptation of a Molière farce. I stuck with debating and the clarinet – did well at the first, winning local and national competitions, and continued to be terrible at the latter, although I enjoyed being part of the school orchestra and wind band.

I still measured myself against the absence of my sister – where she had been head girl, I was appointed deputy. My grades – while good enough to get me into Edinburgh University like her – fell below the straight As that had booked her a place at the most prestigious medical school in Scotland.

After university, I used to joke that I didn't exist until the BBC came calling. Anytime my mum was asked, 'How are the girls?' she'd answer, 'They're doing fine. And the elder is a doctor, you know.' Only later did the answer include 'The elder is a doctor, and the younger works for the BBC.' It's an unfair characterisation, as my parents have always been tremendously supportive of all our successes, however big or small, while trying to teach us the values that go beyond competition.

When I was really into squash and pushing hard to be included in the Scotland squad for my age group, I remember being enormously frustrated by my mum: she restricted the number of ranking competitions I could enter because they were held over two days at weekends. We had a standing commitment to church on Sunday, which could not simply be set aside when something shinier came along. That, and being told between games, in a match where I was spectacularly annoyed with myself for having an off-day, 'You will *never* be a worthy winner if you can't be a good loser', set the tone for success to be worked at and striven for. But winning was doing your best: it was not a scoreline, and it didn't count if you'd let yourself or others down in the process.

Beyond the sister I could never match, the women in my life I wanted to impress were my teachers. We all have special ones who resonate down the years, and I remember mine: Ms Fotheringham, Mrs Glen, Mrs Thomson and Mrs Reid. Mrs Reid, my English teacher and debating coach, came to our house before I left for university to drop off the present of a book. It was a biography of Robert Burns (I used to tease her about her Burns obsession, preferring in my overwrought teenage years the tragic romanticism of Keats). Inside the cover she'd written a line from Shakespeare: 'There is a tide in the affairs of men . . .' The speech goes on:

Which, taken at the flood, leads on to fortune.
Omitted, all the voyage of their life
Is bound in shallows and in miseries.
On such a full sea are we now afloat.

Underneath she'd added, 'This could be it!' At the time I thought she'd meant 'Take all opportunities that present themselves to you. Don't be afraid to leap.' Now I'm not sure it wasn't more a case of 'Don't fuck it up', given how lost I became in my student years. But I'd like to think I've pulled some of it back with decisions taken and opportunities hazarded since.

But to me, those women were instructors, inspirers, mentors, even. They weren't role models. I didn't want to *be* them. I just wanted not to let them down.

I never understood why people needed to see someone like them achieve in order to believe that, some day, they might too. To me, if you want to do something, give it your best crack, and if you fail, either try again or try something else.

All of that changed when I won the leadership of the Scottish Conservatives. As the youngest and least experienced person to go forward for the role, I started from miles behind. But I worked hard over many months during the campaign and was ready to get stuck in when I squeaked through in the vote. At the time, the party was coming out of two decades of under-performance in Scotland, was roundly ridiculed or dismissed in the press, and had endured yet another poor national election result just a few months before. We were dismissed by journalists and commentators alike as either ineffective or – worse – irrelevant to the debate.

In that context, what happened next surprised me. I started getting emails. Mostly from young gay men, but some from young gay women, almost all starting 'I'm not a Conservative, but . . .' They went on to talk about how they were so pleased to see me win the leadership as a gay woman. A number said they were not out yet in their school or to their families – or they were out and were getting bullied. Some were incredibly personal, others absolutely heartbreaking. But the message in all of them was that these young people were interested in politics but thought it was something they could never do because of their sexuality. It mattered to them to see someone gay take on a national leadership role.

Until that point, it had never occurred to me – never so much as crossed my mind – that anyone outside the member-ship of the party would give a fig who the leader was. That it would impact on anyone beyond the members and activists. But now dozens of young people had poured their hearts out because they'd seen something they'd never thought would or could happen, and it had given them some sort of hope.

Despite the madness of taking over the reins of a fractious party, I made sure I replied personally to every single one of the emails I received, often in quite personal terms about my own situation and what it had been like for me growing up. It is to the credit of each of those young people that not one of my responses ever found its way into the newspapers. And it made me realise that I had a responsibility to people outside my immediate sphere. The good Presbyterian that I am, this responsibility manifested itself in a mantra of 'Just don't be shit, and don't let anybody down.' If I just worked hard and didn't mess up, then even if someone didn't share my politics, at least I wouldn't embarrass them. I wouldn't let gay people down. I put huge pressure on myself and, when there was an inevitable mistake, I would beat myself up mercilessly, often not sleeping as I turned an ill-advised comment or missed opportunity over and over in my head, mentally punishing myself for the slip.

Those emails made me think, too, about people's perceptions of politicians. I promised myself that – although I didn't want to be known as 'the gay politician' because I had so much more to say – I would never shrink from or duck questions about my sexuality. I would never tell a journalist such questions were off-limits. If there was something I didn't want to answer, I would explain why – to protect my loved ones or because the question would not be acceptable to a straight person and I wanted to be treated the same as everybody else.

I also made it my mission to keep repeating in every interview that, under my leadership, the Tory Party needed representatives from all backgrounds. I didn't care how old you were, whether you were male or female, straight or gay, which school you went to, what job you did, the only thing I cared about – the only thing – was your commitment to your community and your belief in service. Some people need to see the barriers fall before they give something a shot.

For women, we see persistent inequities: the stubborn gender pay gap, the narrowing of the pyramid in an industry where large numbers of women start but senior management is dominated by men. We see the figures for women on company boards and scan the list of CEOs of the world's biggest firms and confirm that more than half of the world's population has but a fraction of the representation.

The tools adopted by different countries and companies to remedy this are myriad: mentorship and networking schemes, gender-blind hiring practices, quota systems, shared parental leave, equal-pay legislation, a right to flexible working. Yet still a woman entering the world of work in the UK today can expect to earn hundreds of thousands less during her working life than a man entering the same occupation.

The gender pay gap is closing, but women starting out in the world of work now can still expect to earn significantly less than their male contemporaries over their working lives. There are more female than male applicants for UK medical schools, but the ranks of consultants are still overwhelmingly male.

And in politics, we see role models in almost every British political party and parliament. As I write, women simultaneously hold the offices of prime minister, first minister of Scotland, first minister of Northern Ireland, and the leaderships of Plaid Cymru, the Welsh Liberal Democrats, the Scottish Conservatives, Sinn Féin and the Alliance Party in Northern Ireland, along with the co-convenerships of the UK and Scottish Green parties. And yet, and yet . . . The number of women in elected politics remains dwarfed by that of men.

The parties approach the issue differently. Labour has adopted all-female shortlists, although there is a debate around allowing people who were born male but self-identify as female to be included. The Conservatives have chosen a mentorship scheme, which identifies, recruits, supports and assesses women as they seek election. Both have had their successes, but while numbers have increased, we're still a long way from parity.

The rise of women's networks and mentorship schemes in workplaces across the world are designed to open the pipeline to women entering senior and executive roles. Seeing someone blaze a trail can encourage those who come after.

The rower Dame Katherine Grainger is the UK's most decorated female Olympian, having won medals at five consecutive summer Olympic Games. But she started in the sport late – picking up her first oar at university. It was her time as a student that convinced her international competition was possible, in no small part because a recent graduate from the same rowing club had already qualified for Team GB.

❝ *A girl called Dot Blackie who had been at Edinburgh – she grad- uated before me – was the first female captain of the boat club. She had this incredible reputation. I didn't know her, but I'd heard of her. She brought the whole team up to where it should have been. She ruled with an iron fist but in an amazing, inspi- rational way. Her photo was everywhere around the boat club.*

She had gone on to be on the Olympic team, she'd been at Atlanta in 1996. There's something about someone having been in the boathouse I'd been in, the gym I'd been at, the boat I'd sat in, the rowing machine I'd used, and now being in the Olympic team. That became a link.

I went to the British trial at Henley with one of the other girls. We boated the wrong way. We put the boat into the water in the way we'd always done it on the Edinburgh canal, and a lovely guy who used to work for the British rowing team came up and was like 'Oi, Jocks, you're going the wrong way.' We were basically about to row in the wrong direction. Not a great start.

After, I remember walking with Jo (the girl I was with) and we saw Dot Blackie and were like 'It's Dot Blackie! The legend!' She was talking to the rest of the Olympians and, as we walked behind her, she just leaned back without looking at us and said, 'Well done, Edinburgh,' because we'd done quite well in the trial. We just thought, God! She knows who we are! Those little moments, they start building your confidence. You think, Oh, my God, this could be possible.

And at the end of my fourth year, we both rowed for Great Britain. I was then twenty-three and we medalled, so that was a successful first summer. And, suddenly, we were part of this whole new generation, and I was on the team with Dot Blackie. It was just amazing.

Sheila Marcelo is the founder and CEO of Care.com, the world's largest online destination for finding and managing family care. It has 28.4 million members across twenty countries and is one of only twenty-seven S&P 500 companies with a female CEO. Not content to be a trailblazer, Marcelo founded WomenUp. org to increase women's roles in the global economy through leadership training, mentorship and support. With so few female executives, she has co-opted men to help with the programme.

It's important for me to continue playing a role, to press forward and advise people around the challenges I've faced.

What I'm trying to do now is encourage more men to mentor women because there aren't enough female mentors and role models. I think it's important that the few female leaders who have founded or scaled companies become role models for other women, but I do think men need to play that role too. Just like men played it for me in my life. I wouldn't be where I am today if I hadn't had the terrific male mentors that I had.

They asked me to give a speech for women leaders at the World Economic Forum and I was inspired to create WomenUp. org when I asked the women to stand and had the men look up at them. I realised that if we had programmes to support women's confidence, women's advancement, women's ability to get promotion, and more men helping to pull women up, things would really change. There are so few of us doing mentoring around female leadership and female entrepreneurship. I had conversations with male CEOs, many of them my friends. They know that they will attract female and male graduates 50:50, but years down the line there aren't enough senior women and those male CEOs say, 'What's going on? What can we do?'

Then I co-founded a company called Landed with another female entrepreneur, Lisa Skeete Tatum. Landed is a platform to help women advance in the workplace through personal coaching, branding, mentoring, access to jobs and competency scoring. It's a wonderful tool that's selling itself to companies interested in investing in women, and many male CEOs are backing it. It's been gratifying to see ways in which my entrepreneurial journey can help other female leaders and to come up with new solutions to help women.

On the debate that's happening around the world regarding female quotas for boards, Marcelo 's views have changed:

I used to be biased against quotas and thought it [more equal representation on company boards] should just naturally happen if we had the support system. I do think that if we waited that long to have them build the tools, it would take us fifty to a hundred years. So sometimes I think that the quotas could move towards better role modelling and more advancement, raising awareness and removing barriers that make it so hard to advance.

Now, as a CEO, I see the biases. Quotas don't necessarily indicate that the merit of the individual who has to fill a board seat is compromised. Not in any way. I don't think quotas indicate poor-quality candidates – I've heard that argument and I don't believe it – because the pipeline is full of very qualified women.

Tina Brown became editor of her first magazine, *Tatler*, at just twenty-five. Going on to edit *Vanity Fair* and the *New Yorker*, her management style has been shaped by her own experiences in newsrooms across the globe, and by her husband, former editor of *The Times* Harold Evans. She believes that, even once women reach the top, the rules for female bosses are different from those for males.

I do think that women have to work four times as hard, there's no doubt about it. I know plenty of men who have been knocked off their perches who are instantly rehired, instantly given something commensurate. But that never happens to women.

There was a Rockefeller study recently into Fortune 500 companies. It said if they have women CEOs and if the company goes wrong and they are fired, they are never hired again. And I think that's really interesting. It's not true of the men. If they have a failure, sometimes it's a career ruiner, but more often than not they get something else. It may be a smaller company to run or whatever, but they still get rehired. The women never do. So it's like you get your shot, and if it doesn't work, people don't come back. I see that happening again and again.

I have always hired a lot of women and I have a lot of great women in my circle who have worked for or with me. I like to feel that I extend myself for other women. I think I do. But I don't do it self-consciously and think, Oh, I should mentor. I hate the obsession with mentoring. I think that mentoring is a really weird new concept. Training is one thing, mentoring is another. The idea behind mentoring is that you always give somebody positive reinforcement, but sometimes mentoring should mean giving them negative feedback too. Sometimes you have to say, 'That's not good enough, do it differently.'

The people who trained me to be who I am said, 'Do it again.' If I put my husband back into being the great editor that he is and say, 'What's this like? What do you think?' he'll say, 'The pagination stinks.' Or 'What the hell's this on the cover? I don't

understand that. I can't read the title.' And you want that,
right? I don't want him to say, 'Oh, it's fabulous,' all the time.
I'm lucky to have him, because he's always been my mentor.

The idea of *needing* a quota really grates on me. It offends my inner feminist – that spaces should have to be set aside or special accommodation afforded to women just because of their gender. I want to scream a massive 'fuck you' to a system that says we must ration and apportion seats at the decision-making table because, without such dispensation, women wouldn't be able to take those seats on their own. But I cannot fault the change in thought process women like Sheila Marcelo have made. From thinking, like me, there is something inherently wrong (perhaps even demeaning or defeatist) in the require-ment for such set-aside placings, to recognising that the outcome is more important than the journey. If quotas lead to all the other ways of opening doors – creating more role models, allowing for more mentoring, encouraging a critical mass of new entrants, supporting greater company networks – perhaps they can speed that journey up. I'm conflicted as to whether that is an admission of defeat, or simply a practical tool. It is certainly true that there are plenty of qualified women out there, not all of whom find themselves able to access roles reflecting their experience and ability.

DAME KATHERINE GRAINGER
Olympian

British rower Dame Katherine Grainger is a 2012 Summer Olympics gold medallist, four-times Olympic silver medallist and six-times world champion. Grainger holds an LLB from the University of Edinburgh, an MPhil in medical law and medical ethics from the University of Glasgow, in addition to a PhD in law from King's College London. In 2015 she was named chancellor of Oxford Brookes University, and in April 2017 she was appointed chair of development organisation, UK Sport.

❝ In a boat, you're with these people more than you're with any members of your family or your partner. It's usually six or seven days a week – and that's if you're in the UK. If you're abroad, it's constant, 24/7.

When you're away, you share rooms, eat together, train together, and you don't get much time away from each other. And when you're back here – even though we all live separately and escape – all day, every day is with each other.

The first pair I was in, I was with a girl called Cath. She sat in front of me and, after a time, I knew even from the slight movement of her shoulders what mood she was in or what she would say. You can read people, and it's part of the job, really. You learn so much about your sporting partners, what will put them up and what down, what you need to say to motivate them. If you say something and there is a slight movement or bristle, you think, That was wrong, or That was right.

One of the things I was good at was adjusting. I could usually complement. If you're with someone incredibly laid back, you need to be a bit more 'Right, come on.' Or if you've got someone who's really full-on, you need to help them unwind and relax. You constantly need to adapt behaviours.

I did it for twenty years. It changed over my career, and I definitely changed as a person. But your skill set develops as well. I could adjust to what was needed most.

Initially, I was in an eight. I was one of the youngest in the crew and was just having a ball. Everyone else was much better and older than me, and I didn't feel I had very much responsibility. It was such fun. Years later, I was speaking to a girl in the crew who does business development. She used that eight to teach the different roles people can play in any organisation. I was slightly fearful – 'What do you say about me?' She replied, 'You never realised it, but your role was absolutely crucial. Everyone else was so serious, so focused, and you defused everything without understanding what you were doing.'

After I'd done two Olympics, I wondered, How do I keep going? What else is there to do? Eventually a coach sat me down and said, 'You haven't done the stroke seat.' That's the traditional leadership seat. 'You should take that on . . .'

I took it for the next two Olympics, and it brought a different responsibility. Every seat is crucial in a boat – you cannot have a weak seat and you cannot have a weak performance – but in that seat I said to myself, 'Now you are a leader in every sense, on and off the water.' **"**

SHEILA MARCELO
Founder, chairwoman and CEO, Care.com

Sheila Marcelo founded Care.com in 2006. Today, her business is the largest online care provider in the world, matching 28.4 million people across twenty countries with care professionals. Sheila's inspiration to found Care.com came from her own life experience. A Filipina-American squeezed at an early age between care for two small children and ailing parents, she was challenged to find care and knew technology was the answer. Her determination has built a multimillion-dollar global business that has enabled millions of families to get back to work.

“ My mom was very driven. What's interesting is, she got married so young that she became an entrepreneur. She didn't fulfil her life's dream. She originally wanted to be a lawyer so I feel like my mom is living vicariously through me and constantly pushing me to achieve my dreams, which has been incredibly gratifying and inspirational to have someone being so supportive.

What's great about being raised in the Philippines is that it has one of the narrowest gender gaps in the Asian countries. It's a matriarchal culture, and in pre-colonial times we allowed women to be priestesses and to own land so it's in the culture of the country. But I also believe it's got an incredible care infrastructure. There are amazing women and caregivers, and Filipinas are known as amazing caregivers around the world:

they support other women so they can go to work. And it is really important, because when caregivers go to work, we can *all* go to work.

I believe that if we had the Filipino care infrastructure around the world, it would really help advance women, the way we have experienced it in the Philippines. Having said that, I'm also a big believer in making sure that this profession is sustainable, and certainly developing countries, like the Philippines, have low income, with very low wages for caregivers. We need to address that. If we want a society that advances women, that means all women.

I also think there is a new generation of women. I started to see statistics in Asian countries – it's probably the same in Europe – relating to women who decide not to marry or have children. And it does beg the question: who will take care of the parents of single men? There's always the expectation that women not only care for children but also for both parents and in-laws. And that's going to change. It will force the conversation that men need to play a bigger role in caregiving. It's a mindset that's changing, and the reality of the demographics will hit society fairly hard around its assumptions of those norms. 99

4

To Breed or Not to Breed? That Is the Question

In 2015 the *New Statesman* published a front cover online that caused uproar. It showed the German chancellor, Angela Merkel, Scottish first minister Nicola Sturgeon, Conservative home secretary Theresa May, and Labour leadership contender Liz Kendall grouped around a baby's crib containing no child, just a ballot box. The headline read: 'The Motherhood Trap – why are so many successful women childless?'

Within minutes, criticism flew in to social media: 'disempowering', 'offensive' and 'women once again reduced to their uteri' were some of the more polite comments.

Even one of the featured protagonists – Nicola Sturgeon – chipped in: 'Jeez . . . we appear to have woken up in 1965 this morning!' and later called the image 'crass'.

Many were hurt and confused because of its source. The *New Statesman* is an award-winning current-affairs magazine with at least a hundred years of history and is treated as the in-house journal of the progressive left. How could the right-on feminists at this metropolitan institution turn on the sisterhood and be so, well, *parochial* about it?

The deputy editor, Helen Lewis, to whose work the illustration referred, encouraged doubters to read the article, which contained a sober diagnosis of the choices high-flying women face and how their decisions are judged. 'The piece is about the double bind that women in politics face: if they are mothers, maternity leave and the assumption that they will do most of the childcare can hurt their careers. If they are not, people are often quick to call them selfish, or accuse them of not having a "well-rounded" personality.'

If the *New Statesman* had chosen to publish the article at the same time as it published the cover, not a significant period after the stand-alone image was released, some of the ire might have been muted. But as Fraser Nelson, the editor of the *New Statesman*'s rival publication the *Spectator*, mused, 'Bold, original & provocative @NewStatesman cover this week (ergo causing uproar on Twitter). Suspect it'll sell v well.'

As clickbait, it worked, igniting days of debate across multiple media platforms.

The spark might have been new, but the framing of the debate then and, indeed, now seems continually to relapse into the same old binary categories: either a woman has children or is childless; either she wants them or she doesn't; either she is able to conceive or she can't. It's like the same yes/no flow chart repeated down through history, with men never the focus of the scrutiny.

It's a set of binary equations I've never felt I fitted into. As someone who always thought that *one day* they'd quite like to have children, probably in about five years' time (then realised in my late thirties that a family history of early-onset menopause meant I probably didn't have five years left), it was always a choice for another day. But it was going to be a choice that was made, a decision to be weighed and an action to perform. As a gay woman, whose last romantic overture with a man was so far back in the rear-view mirror it's disappeared over the horizon, the 'Stop taking the pill and, whoops, surprise!' route of family planning has never been an option for me.

I have always felt that when it came to children, so many categorisations are black and white, yet somehow I live outside the lines. Because of my sexuality, I've never had to wonder if people are hesitant about hiring me in case I go off on maternity leave: the very clear assumption and expectation has been that if I'm gay and childless that will continue.

And yet, and yet . . . For all the black and white, I feel as if I'm writing this book in an enormous swathe of grey: I'm writing it largely while pregnant, having gone through an IVF process that was, at times, invasive, joyous, mortifying, fearful and hopeful. There is a special feeling of wanting the earth to swallow you whole when you are led in a hospital gown to the room where an internal examination is going to take place by a nurse who decides to strike up conversation with 'I saw you on the telly last night, talking about the NHS.'

There is also a particular challenge in trying discreetly to sort out the various appointments and treatments, while keeping up the pace of political leadership, so no one suspects that anything's going on. It leads to some interesting situations, such as having to stab yourself in the stomach with hormone injections in the oddest places – like the toilets at Geneva airport on the way to the World Economic Forum in Davos – or scheduling procedures reliant on your body clock around immovable diary entries. I managed to persuade my embryologist that it would actually be *less* stressful to jump on a plane to Afghanistan a couple of hours after the implantation procedure than go back to the office, because I'd be sitting down, reading briefing notes and watching movies on the in-flight entertainment system. I did suggest to my partner, Jen, that if that cycle worked, we should nickname the bump 'baby Helmand' but we settled on Fionnuala instead.

And while the debate on high-flying career women having children is still cast as a series of binary choices, people's lives don't fit neatly into those boxes.

I chose the women to interview for this book because of their achievements – they are either the first women to perform the role they hold or have excelled in predominantly male professions. I interviewed none because of their family situations, and none of the interviews focused on the child question. In a number of cases, I was unaware of the nature of my subjects' family set-up as they chose not to mention it so I found little or nothing about it during my research.

But by chance – or perhaps because life doesn't fit neatly in binary boxes – the women featured in this book run from members of the conventional nuclear family of mum, dad and two kids, to adoptive parents, to women who have chosen not to have children, to those who are unable to conceive, to gay parents, single parents and, finally, to a mum who used an egg donor and surrogate to allow her to start a family.

Every one of them is different and their situations are distinct, but each faces challenges in family life. Their experiences show that those challenges may be professional or personal, but with children or without, they have still been able to reach the top.

By the end of her thirties, media mogul Tina Brown had rejuvenated *Tatler* and *Vanity Fair*, and modernised the *New Yorker*. She'd also had two children with her husband, Harold Evans, twenty-five years her senior. She describes them both as workaholics. Brown is the founder of the news website Daily Beast, and Women in the World, which brings together female leaders from around the globe at live journalism events. An award-winning journalist and best-selling author, she says it's her children she's most thankful for. For some women – though not for all – family is everything.

" *It's all about who you go home to. I have a fabulous husband – so sane and loving and supportive and funny – and these two wonderful children. I have a boy who has Asperger's, and it has been hugely enlarging to have a kid who has all these challenges. It's bonding for the family to go with him on his journey and every small achievement for him is a huge thing for us.*

He's now thirty and is doing very well. In the last year I was so proud of him – he's now living in his own apartment and he works three days a week at a non-profit organisation. He loves it and is so proud. He's been transformed by having this job and his independence, and it's just wonderful. It's so gratifying to have a child who goes through these things. It is enormously grounding. All this other stuff, I would just trade it, for him.

My daughter is absolutely wonderful. She went to Harvard and now she's at Vice News. She's working to be a producer on a new show. She's incredibly empathetic and sweet because of her brother and is so kind and lovely to him. Those are the things that matter. For me, I go up, I go down – it doesn't matter. I've still got all of that. It really is all about who you go home to.

In 2004, tech pioneer Baroness Martha Lane Fox had recently stepped down as MD of lastminute.com, the online business she had built and sold for over half a billion pounds, and was preparing for her next commercial role. During a visit to Morocco, a life-changing accident left her – along with many broken bones – subject to horrific internal injuries. In 2016, Martha announced she was the proud mother of twin boys, born to a surrogate in the US.

It was the only option. I didn't have a womb after the accident and didn't have any eggs left, so we used an egg donor and a surrogate. We tried the UK, but it didn't work, so we went to America.

We put one embryo into Heidi, our amazing surrogate, and it split – so that was a surprise. We hadn't quite remembered our biology. Thank God, though, because it is an amazing experience to watch identical twins emerge into the world.

And now, two years in, I feel like 'Okay, I'm getting it now.' I'm beginning to understand this stuff. For the first two years I was all over the place.

It goes round in my head a bit. My husband is adopted so it's not like these scenarios are completely outside my comfort zone. My best friend adopted her kids, so I've had a few examples. Sometimes I think it feels a bit different from that, from the set models for adoption, but I genuinely don't feel anxious about it. I feel 'Wow, they're here,' and this is just extraordinary. Hopefully I can do my best by them and not make it a strange journey but an extraordinary one. My concern is less about me and more about making it easy for them.

I feel so lucky to live in a time when in 2018 two amazing women can help me have two children – how extraordinary is that?

Dame Katherine Grainger has been an elite athlete for a quarter of a century; her focus on her sport was absolute. She is a doting aunt and acts as godmother to the children of several former crewmates, none of whom returned to racing after motherhood. With no mother ever having competed internationally for Great Britain at rowing, the choice was children or the job. Now forty-two, Katherine says she's got some choices of her own to make.

There is an age by which, if you haven't had children, it becomes 'Will you have them? Do you still want them? Why haven't you had them? Have you thought about it? Have you not thought about it?' I don't know if it irritates me. I suppose you accept it as inevitable: people are interested.

I grew up in a happy family, my mum, dad, sister and me, and although divorce rates are quite high, all my friends grew up in that unit. So I grew up expecting that, at some point, I would have kids as that was normal to me. But I never thought I'd end up with the path I've gone down and I obviously never could have had kids while I was competing.

At some point it won't be a choice: when you haven't made the choice, 'yes' or 'no', it's suddenly made for you. I've not ruled it out. I'm not saying, 'I just don't want kids,' because I love them.

And then I get to the point of asking if I would have changed any of it. I could have stopped after Beijing, Athens, London. If I'd had kids then, my life would have been very different. You'd gain and you'd lose.

I probably don't have a definitive answer. I'm getting to the point where I'm going to run out of time and I'm not actively doing anything about it. Maybe it's a bit like when I didn't know what I would do career-wise post-London or post-Rio. You sort of keep yourself very busy to avoid the tricky questions. I'm probably a bit guilty of that.

Eventually my mum will make me do it as she wants more grandchildren. She's the one who always asks the hard personal questions. So that's the mother–daughter conversation that will be coming.

Grainger is not the only person for whom the decision around having children equates to arresting her career. The broadcaster Sandi Toksvig was already a household name when she came out as gay. As a children's TV presenter, writer and comedienne, she was forced into hiding along with her family after she received death threats for having had children within a same-sex relationship.

It was very difficult to meet people, so I went to an evening discussion at a place called Gay's the Word and met Peta, who is the mother of my children. We were together for a long time. She was desperate to have kids and we had three – very secret, very quiet – but when I came out all hell broke loose.

I came out because in the end I had to protect my kids from having secrets. I had to sacrifice my career – that was what I was told. It's not that long ago – 1994. I was told I'd never work again. It's still very painful to think about it.

The Daily Mail *whipped up a complete storm of hatred. The headline on the front page was 'If God had meant lesbians to have children he'd have made it possible.' Well, we did have children and clearly it was possible – so that didn't make sense.*

We had death threats. We had to take the kids into hiding. They were very graphic, the threats. We didn't know anybody else, any other lesbians, with children. We were terrified that the authorities would take them from us. So we were being threatened and were terrified – and the threats were credible.

*And I didn't know if anyone would support me. I felt the lone-
liest and most terrified I've ever felt in my life.*

*You sit by your child's bed when you're in hiding and think,
What have I done? Because you just love them so much. I'd have
given up everything for them. Not a problem. I just wanted to
protect them and look after them. We were terrified of accessing
official protection. Now I would go straight to the police.*

*The things I do remember that were extraordinary: the head-
mistress at the girls' primary school was fantastic – Mrs Walton.
She was amazing. There was a playground at the front, which
could be seen from the street, and a playground at the back, so
she arranged for the kids to play at the back. And just moved
everything around. She put the kids first and was incredible. I'll
always be grateful to her.*

*That was the week Save the Children dropped me as an
ambassador. I'd been a long-time ambassador and they dropped
me. So, save the kids – but not the gay ones . . . Three weeks
ago I met the chief executive of Save the Children and he apologised. It made me cry. Twenty-four years, it took.*

Toksvig's experiences with her family, and the fear she felt
about the possibility of her children being taken away, prompted
her to seek protection under the law. Her then partner might
have been the birth-mother of her children, but Toksvig wanted
to be recognised as their parent. Her legal fight broke new
ground for same-sex couples in England.

*I've had various death threats down the years. I now go straight
to the hate-crime squad, who I'm on kissing terms with. Many of*

them are in the Gay Men's Chorus, so they sang at my wedding. I have no issues now about making the biggest noise, and the police have done wonderful things to people who have threatened me. I adore them and think they're fabulous.

But it took a lot of courage – Peta and I were the first lesbian couple to get a court order to make sure that the kids were mine. Because there was no gay marriage or civil partnerships.

I remember going to court and this wonderful woman judge said, 'I give this order and nothing has ever given me greater pleasure.' It was just phenomenal. And once I'd got that bit of paper I didn't care any more what anyone said because no one was going to take the kids from me. But nobody knew we were going to get that kind of legal backing to say, 'Yeah, they are absolutely your kids.'

They are fabulous and I would never do it differently. If I had to give up every single thing – that I have, that I do, that I am – for the benefit of my children, I would do it without a single thought. They are amazing. But it would have been great to have known just one other lesbian couple at the time – we didn't know anyone. It would have made such a difference.

The old adage that children change your life was certainly true for Sheila Marcelo. She and her husband, Ron, met at a cross-college function for Filipino students studying in the US. Early in their relationship, Sheila found herself pregnant. Unmarried and thousands of miles from home, she didn't have access to a support structure. When her second son arrived – also unexpectedly – she founded Care.com, the world's largest care marketplace.

I was born and raised in the Philippines and I came to America for college. I got pregnant between my sophomore and junior years. My husband and I were not expecting that. He wasn't yet my husband, so shortly after we heard we were pregnant, we got married.

Being from a Catholic family, it was very difficult. His parents were deceased and mine were in the Philippines so we didn't really have a lot of care options for our son, Ryan. Then – fast-forward to when we were in graduate school – we had another unexpected gift. His name is Adam.

We asked my parents in the Philippines to come over and help us care for him. When my father was carrying him up the stairs, he fell backwards and had a heart attack. So at twenty-nine, I was working at a technology company but finding carers through the Yellow Pages *for children and seniors.*

I was sandwiched, and I realised so many other families, millions of them, needed solutions to find care. So my own personal experience inspired me. Today Care.com is actually helping caregivers find jobs to match with families, and at the same time we also provide a financial platform, handling payroll, payments, social security and other benefits for caregivers.

Your care needs are constantly changing. Sometimes it takes you longer to look for something because you may have a specific need. You may need full-time and later you'll go to part-time care because your children are in school. They're different needs. If you're looking for senior or special-needs care, those are different needs. We made it more flexible for families to decide what they want to do.

We have seen from the get-go that this is a two-sided

marketplace: the supply side with caregivers and, on the demand side, families seeking care. What was so interesting is that there is a huge overlap of women on both sides. So at least 90 per cent of our caregivers are women, and in about 85 per cent of our families, the chief household officer, primarily responsible for seeking care in the family, is the woman.

Still in the grey area of being pregnant but not having given birth, I have no idea how changing family responsibilities will affect the way I do my job. What has been interesting, though, has been the reaction to the announcement. While plenty of male political leaders – including multiple prime ministers while in office in Downing Street – have had children and made choices about paternity leave, no female politician in the UK has ever started a family and taken maternity leave while leading a party. I didn't know what the reaction would be when I announced it – particularly with the complicating factor of my being in a same-sex relationship (this pregnancy was not unplanned). In fact, media and political responses have been overwhelmingly positive – especially when contrasted with Sandi Toksvig's experience outlined above. Perhaps this will make it easier and less remarkable for future female political leaders to start a family during their period in office, as well as showing that society is far less proscriptive – and far more accepting – of the different choices women make.

Baroness Lane Fox of Soho is a prominent businesswoman, public servant and philanthropist. She is best known for co-founding lastminute.com during the early 2000s, the period known as the 'dot-com boom'. Later she sold the travel website for £577 million, and now sits on the board of Twitter in addition to chairing the digital skills charity Go ON UK. In March 2016, she was appointed to the House of Lords, where she sits as a cross-bench peer.

" I often think that if people who have been successful say that they haven't had a massive amount of luck, they are not telling the truth.

I wasn't a technologist by background. I was a classical historian. I just loved the power of what the new was creating and that was what appealed to me. At twenty-one, it felt like fun. It was the vanguard of an industry and, as with most things, we learned on the fly.

But when I look back to those early days at lastminute.com, it wasn't the tech sector I remember as brutal when I was the youngest or the only woman. It was more the interactions we had with the finance industry or even the travel industry, where it was more shocking.

Tech didn't have any women, but finance and travel had them in all these junior roles, then none at any level where I would be meeting people as the founder of a business that banks were trying to court, or as somebody negotiating with the head of sales of an airline. I remember thinking, This is just extremely odd.

I remember trying to get airline seats from Lufthansa, being in meetings with a very bureaucratic, old-fashioned German company – never unkind – and just feeling like a total outlier and constantly having to think, How am I going to get my point across and be credible?

Later on, when I was setting up the government digital service and building gov.uk, in a way that was more entrepreneurial than lastminute.com had been, I had to be on a massive charm offensive across the civil service, across the political class. I had sixteen ministerial meetings, sixteen head of department meetings, went to so many subcommittees of the cabinet.

That was when I felt depressed that I was often one of only one or two women in the room. That is a different kind of power dynamic. If it is your own business, it has a different kind of energy and motivation. But when you are trying to get something done in those huge bureaucracies, it felt as though it wasn't always in their interests to follow your lead.

I recently joined the Joint Committee on the National Security Strategy, partly because the world of defence has changed so dramatically. I'm not a cyber expert, but I'm interested in how you can apply the same logic to the digital disruption that's happened and how we face defence. I also thought, I bet there are not many women in this industry and I'm really interested to understand it better.

In a debate in the House of Lords recently on defence, I was the only woman speaking out of thirty-two people. I turned to the peer sitting next to me and said, 'I can't believe this. It's the second time I've spoken in a debate and I'm the only woman.' And he looked at me and said, 'Well, it's not a very girly subject.'

I wanted to punch him in the face. How could we still be having that conversation? **"**

TINA BROWN
Journalist and publisher

Arguably the first celebrity editor and one of the most influential figures in journalism, Tina Brown's contact book remains unparalleled. Her time at the helm of Vanity Fair *and the* New Yorker *revolutionised both publications and shook up the publishing industry in America.*

❝ I was a freelance writer. I was writing all over the place and I came to realise that I was really annoyed with the assignments I was getting and the people who were editing me. I kept feeling I had better ideas but couldn't get them through. They made me think I should have my own magazine, but I never thought anyone would give me one. Then along came this wacky Australian who had bought the *Tatler* and he was looking for an editor. He asked to meet me and we got along and he said, 'Why don't you edit it?'

It was a sort of society rag that had silly old ladies and no wider reception. I just thought it was an opportunity. That it was moribund just meant, okay, clean slate, but it was still a title that had existed for 270 years. I just blindly set out to do it. I hired all my friends and there we were: we were real *enfants terribles*, tykes throwing mud against the wall.

Everybody on the magazine was about 190. It was so old, and I thought, Let's change the society it covers, because the society it was covering were the old tweedy Scots lords. Instead I thought, Let's cover the *real* society.

Princess Diana was rising – it was a mouse-that-roared moment. She was only a couple of years younger than most of my staff and we got to cover that story and rode it to the max. Diana was our feast: we profiled the people who dressed her, the people who did her hair, the places where she ate, what she did, her friends. It became like a fabulous soap opera for us and we did very well with it.

I saw myself as lucky to have a platform. I love responding to the news and having a voice. I'd thought I had no opinions, but then I realised I was full of them. I like to express myself, and having a magazine was just a fantastic playground for me. And to be given first the *Tatler* and then *Vanity Fair* . . . I consider myself enormously lucky.

With *Vanity Fair* it was an incredibly exciting moment in magazines in America. I had a budget, I had a staff, I had a fabulous company behind me. I had a boss who really appreciated me and backed me, gave me enough funds to do what I wanted and left me alone. He never interfered with my opinions or my hires, or anything I wanted to publish. And with the *New Yorker*, we brought it back from the dead and changed the demographic. Our regime came in and we saved the *New Yorker*, I can honestly say that.

It's only when you are out of something that you realise you were in a Camelot at that particular moment. It was a golden time, and I realise it more and more because I am now looking at a decimated media. It really does break my heart to see that there are 40 per cent fewer reporters than there were at the last election. I was lucky enough to have wonderful writers working for me and time to do the pieces. I could commission the writers to do something, and I could pay them properly so that they could do it. That's gone and I'm mourning. I mourn my profession. **"**

Men vs Women

How are men treated differently from women?

I have spent almost all of my adult working life in male-dominated environments, whether newsrooms, parliaments or army barracks. I've lost count of the number of times I've found myself as the only woman in the room, or round the decision-making table.

I have never struggled to contribute in such situations, to have my voice heard or my ideas given proper consideration. I like and appreciate men – just not enough to marry one.

But I do sometimes wonder if I've been short-changed, as the bosses I've responded to best, or wanted to go the extra mile for, have both been female: my programme editor at the BBC, and my predecessor as Scottish Conservative leader. Could I have developed faster or requested more responsibility earlier if I'd had a few more senior women to show me the way?

According to the TUC, more than half of the women in the

UK have experienced some form of sexual harassment in the workplace, and UK government figures confirm 90 per cent of sectors pay full-time working women less than men. Such results have contributed to the UK falling four places in the World Economic Forum's gender-gap rankings in just five years.

While I know this is not everyone's experience, I've struggled to remember a time when, as a woman, I've been talked to differently in any workplace – at least not a time that I'm aware of (it may have happened and I just bulldozed my way through it without thinking). Nor do I believe my performance has been routinely assessed on a different scale from that of male colleagues.

The disciplines I've chosen have always had their own intrinsic measure. In politics, you're elected if more people vote for you than for the other candidates, and all votes weigh the same. As a political leader, your ability to stay in post is broadly – though not exclusively – dependent on how many seats your party can win in national elections.

In the army, annual assessments – in navigation, battlefield casualty drills, operational law, chemical and biological warfare drills, personal-weapon training – are gender-blind. Even the load in the annual combat-fitness test – marching eight miles in two hours, carrying between fifteen and twenty-five kilos of kit plus your weapon – is decided by your regiment, not your sex.

At the BBC, audience figures come in every quarter, so you can see how popular or otherwise individual programmes are. I spent the lion's share of my time at the Corporation working on a news and current-affairs radio programme. Broadcast every day between four and six p.m., two people presented it, and there were four of us on the roster. On the days we weren't in the hot

seat, we helped the production and research team. The work –
deciding which stories to cover, setting up guests, writing scripts
and conducting interviews – was not physical. Yet it is the only
time I've felt I've been treated differently for being female.

A few years into my stint, one of my male co-presenters
decided to take a sabbatical year abroad and kindly let me
know his salary before he left. It was more than a third greater
than I was earning for the same role. Granted, he had been
there a couple of years longer, but that was still a big difference.

I didn't sleep before my meeting with the department head
– my boss's boss's boss. I had no idea what to say or how to
say it. I'd grown up in a Presbyterian household where you
just didn't talk about money. It was embarrassing, almost
shameful, to do so. What if they fired me? Or moved me to
another, lesser, role to match my wages? Somehow I stumbled
out the issue and that I didn't think it was right. I was told all
the reasons why it wasn't possible to make up the difference
– budgets were tight, it was above the percentage increase
allowed for annual rises across the department, and was told
it was really an HR matter. I argued that I had already consulted
HR, who had referred me to the head of news. He sucked his
cheeks and offered me half the difference – a five-figure sum
that would have made a huge difference to my life. I got up
and walked out.

I couldn't believe I'd been offered the single biggest pay rise
of my entire life – for no extra work – and I'd turned it down. I
cursed myself for being stupid all the way home, thinking of
what those extra hundreds each month could pay for. Maybe I
could move out of my shared flat and get a place of my own,

where I didn't find all the milk drunk in my absence. But a principle was at stake, and I countered to myself that I hadn't been outrageous. I wasn't arguing for the full amount or for back pay, I just wanted to be paid closer to what my male colleague received.

Two weeks later I found myself in front of the head of news once again. He upped the offer a few thousand more until it was three-quarters of the difference of my co-presenter's wage. It seemed a fair enough recognition of his length of service and increased experience, and I agreed on the spot. It also struck me how asymmetric the negotiation had been: I was arguing for the only money I received. I had no other means, no savings or other employment. I lived for three weeks out of every month on my overdraft, and even one small economic shock would have left me in real trouble. It *mattered* to me what I was paid: all the other things in my life depended on it.

It did not particularly matter to the boss if I got paid the same as someone else or not. He had hundreds of people under him and – while he had a corporate responsibility to stay within budgets – it wasn't *his* money he was spending. What did it matter to him if one of the team – with whom he'd had only a dozen conversations in four years – was paid X amount or Y? It was so impersonal to the man sitting on one side of the table and the most personal thing in the world to the woman on the other: me.

It still strikes me how powerless I felt – and that was with decades of employment and anti-discrimination law in my corner. I could have been branded a troublemaker and have seen my future prospects hit. I didn't want to work anywhere other than the BBC and, even if I did, nowhere else in the UK would allow me to do what I was doing, which I loved. It was down to the good graces of the department as to whether or not they would agree to pay me more. They could just as easily have said no and the only route to parity would have been through legal action. Which would have killed any chance of promotion stone dead.

One anecdote doesn't make a trend, but new requirements on the BBC to publish the salary brackets of its top stars show that, even fifteen years on from my experience, real discrepancies exist at the other end of the scale from lowly Radio Scotland presenters. At the start of the year, a group of 170 female BBC employees gave a submission to a House of Commons committee accusing the Corporation of breaking equality laws as a result of a 'culture of gender discrimination'. The submission went on to say,

> For many years, women at all levels and in all grades and positions in the BBC both on and off air, staff and freelance, working in the UK and abroad had suspected they were not being paid equally – even when management expressly assured them they were.

> BBC women are very concerned that this publicly funded body is perpetuating a long-standing breach of its stated values of trust, transparency and accountability. We believe the BBC must put these matters right by admitting the problem, apologising and setting in place an equal, fair and transparent pay structure.

The BBC has repeatedly stressed its commitment to equal pay, but since the issue was drawn into the spotlight, the National

Union of Journalists (NUJ) has taken up at least a hundred cases of female BBC employees who believe they are being paid less than their male counterparts.

The NUJ has also written to Parliament, accusing the BBC of 'unnecessary secrecy, a lack of transparency and widespread misuse of managerial discretion', which, it said, had 'clearly normalised an approach to pay that the NUJ believes to be discriminatory and unlawful'.

If you type 'Men vs Women' into an internet search engine, thousands of articles appear. Everything from scholarly studies, published by Ivy League universities, into the cognitive differences between the male and female brains, to college joke pages, to diet guides on how the sexes lose weight differently, to internet filtering tools explaining why men and women prefer different types of porn.

The most striking difference of approach between the sexes ever outlined to me was not about ability, treatment or aptitude, it was about response. Not about the actions that are imposed on women but about how they choose to push back.

Ever since I went to Kosovo as a young journalist, I've kept an interest in the Balkans. A few years ago I travelled to Bosnia with a charity called Remembering Srebrenica to visit the massacre site, learn more about the genocide and bring lessons on stopping internecine hate to communities at home.

Srebrenica was one of a number of enclaves or 'safe zones' held by the UN during the Bosnian war. In return for Bosnian Serb forces refraining from overrunning such zones, Bosniaks – Bosnian Muslims – inside the enclaves were to disarm, and international troops, supplied by the UN, would act as a protection force. In 1995, following a three-year siege, troops under the command of General Ratko Mladić stormed the town, rounded up the male population and started systematically massacring them. Those who tried to escape on foot, in a column now dubbed the 'death march', faced ambush and execution.

In all, more than 8,000 men and boys were slaughtered by Serb forces in the worst atrocity perpetrated on European soil since the Second World War. The International Court of Justice and the European Court of Human Rights have ruled that the killings constituted genocide and, in 2017, Mladić was convicted at the International Criminal Tribunal for the former Yugoslavia at The Hague of war crimes, crimes against humanity and genocide.

But recognition of the atrocity, both at home and internationally, was slow to come. Serb forces tried to cover up their acts, burying the dead in mass graves and often using heavy machinery to dig them up again and redistribute the contents to secondary or tertiary sites. At least ninety such mass graves have been uncovered, with many victims unaccounted for, some impossible to identify and others pieced together: their remains were found in separate places hundreds of miles apart.

There was also unwillingness at the end of the war for those culpable to admit what had occurred. In a region where so much violence had been committed, it was hard for individual acts to receive recognition. But authorities and those responsible for Srebrenica hadn't reckoned on the women of Srebrenica, who had been left behind. Many had been brutalised by the war as Serb soldiers used genocidal rape as part of their programme of ethnic cleansing. But those who had lost fathers, brothers, husbands and sons demanded answers as to what had happened to them. Had they been killed? Where were their bodies? Who was accountable? When could they receive justice?

The mothers of Srebrenica harried and harassed the authorities for years until a true picture of what had occurred was revealed. They succeeded not only in the case of their lost loved ones being taken to international courts more than a decade after the massacre had taken place, but also nearly two decades later they managed successfully to prosecute the Dutch government: Dutch soldiers – serving under the UN flag – had withdrawn from the safe zone when it was overrun by Serb troops and left the populace to their fate.

The mothers, too, were integral to the establishment of a permanent memorial to the massacre and a museum ensuring the story is told. And, at least twenty years after their men were killed, they still meet with international groups who visit the site to give their first-hand accounts of what happened. They will not be silenced.

Following my return to the Balkans I spent several years sitting on the board of the Scottish branch of the Remembering Srebrenica charity and have continued to engage with their work. Just before Mladić's sentencing last year, I led a delegation back to the area. When I met the charity's country director in Bosnia, Rešad Trbonja, he told me that none of what had been done would have been achieved without the women. If it had been the other way round, and the women had been killed, there wouldn't be graves, there wouldn't be names, and no one would know what had happened.

His contention was that if the men had been left, they would have drunk, mourned and fought. But they wouldn't have kept going as the women have. They wouldn't have spoken out.

Although he is a former soldier, who was subjected to terrible violence under horrific conditions during the war, Rešad believes that the women of his country are stronger than he is because they bore violence, privation and loss, and they refused – and keep refusing – to accept such acts being covered up. A quarter of a century on, they are still fighting for the truth to be known and what happened to their husbands, brothers and sons to be recognised, not written out of history.

Seldom is the disparity between women and men so stark as in sport. The most capped male footballer in Europe is Gianluigi Buffon, a goalkeeper who has played 176 times for his native Italy. He is a millionaire many times over and, as well as playing in front of tens of thousands of fans at every match, he is able to command a sizeable income from advertising and sports endorsements. By contrast, Gemma Fay – also a goal-keeper – has been capped 203 times for her country, Scotland. Last year she signed her first, and only, professional contract to finish her club career playing in Iceland. She was paid 1,000 euros a month. At the age of thirty-six, she has combined twenty years of international sport with either full-time education or a full-time job. She's still paying off her student loan. Now retired, Fay says times have changed hugely from when she started her international sporting career, but she doesn't regret her playing days – even if they came without much financial reward.

❝ *It was a bit different in those days. If you were going to be a professional female footballer, you had to play for the US, and the US was like a club team because they just toured. Then they started up the USA Pro League. But you had to be the best of the best.*

In this country and even down south, there weren't full-time professionals. I don't even think there were part-time professionals. England brought in some centralised contracts but that wasn't till later on.

To be honest, I don't think you ever sacrifice anything when you choose to do something. You make a conscious choice, and at times you might not like the choice you made, and it might mean you can't do other things, but that's not a sacrifice if you're choosing.

So, I chose to do what I did. I chose to work. I had opportunities and options to go and play abroad, elsewhere, when I was between twenty-seven and twenty-eight. I had offers from France and Spain. In hindsight, I should have taken them but I didn't – my mother got ill and I was her primary carer. When she passed away I found it really difficult to deal with.

Looking back, I probably used her death as a bit of an excuse because I was scared. I probably hid. And part of that was down to lack of confidence. I didn't really believe in myself. I was scared at twenty-eight to go and play professionally somewhere else because I'd grown up in a family where there wasn't a lot of

*financial stability. I needed to have a job, and playing profes-
sional football was a step into the unknown. What drove me
wasn't financial reward. It was 'Am I good enough? How can I
be better? I need to be better and I need to be good enough.'*

Fay has now changed sports – from football to rugby – and is
in charge of women's rugby in Scotland. She's tasked with
getting more players involved at club level, along with developing the elite game. She's keen that women's sport develops
distinct from male codes, in order to achieve true sustainability.

*When it comes to females versus males in sport, they're
different products and you have to develop them as a product.
Women's football has got a good product now – and we're
starting to see people backing that product and buying into it
and wanting to be associated with it. I see that across women's
sport. There is more investment, but it's taken a while.*

*That's because female sport hasn't been professional for very
long, in comparison with male, and it will take time for that to
develop. I'm not sure it's right just to throw a whole bunch of
money and say, 'It's female sport, you should have the same as
the guys,' because how do you make that sustainable? They did
that with the National Women's Soccer League in America and
it collapsed because there was no market for it.*

*So, it's more about building the market: if you do that you
make it sustainable. You make it attractive. People will want to
watch it, to buy into it, and then it's self-perpetuating.*

> *There's not a magic wand you can wave and say, 'Oh, you're the same as the guys,' – the guys have got seventy, eighty, ninety years' history. It's ingrained within people, within cultures. Women's sport has to be appreciated and valued for what it is.*

Fay believes that women's sport has to be allowed to grow organically – just as male sports have done over history – with the support, attention and promotion of governing bodies serious about the development of the women's game.

As a combat trainer of India's special forces, Dr Seema Rao's daily work means she is the only woman in barrack rooms filled with some of the toughest men on earth. The fact that she's also teaching them how to shoot, fight and kill means the risk is high of bruised egos and over-zealous soldiers keen to prove a point. Despite her slight frame, Dr Rao has spent two decades going toe to toe with those she's instructing – keen to demonstrate her abilities before asking her students to follow suit. It means her body has taken a battering. As a trained doctor, she's acutely aware of her own physical limitations, but is adamant that there is no better way to engender respect and compliance than through direct demonstration.

> *I always lead by positive example, in the sense that I have to keep my skills, strength and techniques honed. Whenever I ask men to do a task, I first demonstrate it to them. And when I actually do it, I think I earn their respect.*
>
> *I also explain the subject to them in a very scientific fashion. I show them a technique and then they have to follow it. I do*

realise that age has a strange way of making things harder, so my husband and I keep training. I keep my body in shape and my skills up – whether that be shooting skills or hand-to-hand combat skills. More than commanding the men, I win their respect by being able to do the task.

I received the news of my father's death when I was on a training assignment. I was teaching the trainees in a grappling session, a wrestling session. It had almost come to an end and somebody ran up to me and told me, 'Your father is no more,' and that I had to leave to go to my city. I was upset, but I wanted to get on with that bout. I landed on my head and was knocked out, concussed. I had amnesia and I took three months to recover. My memory was completely wiped out.

So that was one very bad injury I had. In the second, I fractured my vertebrae. There was a rope slide across two buildings. I was doing a monkey crawl, in which you travel from one end of the rope to the other. So, I was on the rope and it snapped. As I came downwards I hit my back on the wall of the building. There was a sharp pain, like something had cracked, and I had to be taken away on a stretcher, hospitalised. That took about six months.

It was a very bad injury, but something like that was expected. I am a good patient. I understand my body. When there are injuries, I understand I need to rest that part, because the body is signalling what I shouldn't do. I'm patient with my body. And I know when I have to push and when I need to heal.

People say that a man is stronger than a woman, but I say that if a woman works on her physical strength, she can be as strong as a man. When I grapple with my trainees I know exactly how to get them down.

Maria Bello is an award-winning actress, successful producer and committed activist. When she decided she had seen enough movie posters showing two white men hanging out, Bello decided to tackle the disparity – of opportunity and of pay – in Hollywood. With at least forty like-minded artists, producers, agents and executives, she plans to change what movies get made – and who makes them.

It's not unfair at all to see Hollywood as a bunch of white men making decisions about what to portray on the screen. Over the last twelve years only 4 per cent of Hollywood movies have been directed by women. We are working very hard in the Sundance Institute on a new project right now to change that, called the Systemic Change Project.

What's exciting is the way the world is shifting – the way media have exploded through online screening services and YouTube. We are realising that consumers aren't just white males. We're realising that most consumers of TV and film are women. We're seeing that films and TV shows with more diversity make more money. So the needle is shifting in Hollywood because it's good business to have women in front of and behind the camera. It's good business to have diverse characters in front of and behind the camera. Is it slow to happen? Yes. Are we in a position right now to force it to happen? Yes.

In the Systemic Change Project we have peer-to-peer counselling. It's a group of mostly agents, heads of studios, networks, artists, producers, who have gotten together to say enough is enough. Enough saying, 'Oh, poor women. Why aren't we represented?' and instead: 'We're going to change this with action.' That's what I'm really excited about in the women's movement right now: the education and the action. I don't want to talk about things any more. What's the action?

So we have unconscious bias training. Geena Davis instituted this big study at the University of Southern California and found that even in animated films only 30 per cent of characters in the background are women. And when you bring this up with studios, they go, 'Oh, it's not because they're mean guys, it's unconscious.'

There's also a bias about the kind of films women want to see, the old idea of the chick flick. It doesn't exist any more. All of the projects I have right now that I'm producing are women front and forward. I have a project about these incredible women warriors in Africa. Another project is about girls in the Middle East of many different religions who have been taken prisoner by ISIS and share a common enemy, the beauty and truth behind Islam and what it really is. I've got a virtual reality piece about Yazidi women too.

I think that there is such great power in seeing yourself reflected on screen. It validates our experience in so many ways. For young women especially to see themselves on screen, to aspire to something – to realise that they matter, their voice matters – is really, really important.

The television streaming industry is much further ahead of the curve in terms of women and diversity in roles and under-standing what sells. Streaming has opened up huge possibilities for women of every age and every colour to take the lead. It's more affordable to stay home and watch a TV show or some-thing streaming on YouTube than go to a movie theatre. I have a sixteen-year-old, and all he does is watch things on his phone. I think because of that we are seeing more diversity in tele-vision than we are in film.

The wonderful thing is that the Systemic Change Project isn't a group of women: we're a group of men and women who happen to be feminists. We have common values, a common heart and a common goal: what can we do to move this needle forward?

So now we have an ambassador programme, where three of us at a time go to studios, networks and agencies, and in our twenty-minute spiel, not only do we talk about unconscious gender bias training, but a gender parity stamp. So, at the end of a film you may see a stamp, and to get that stamp a movie needs four out of eight points: a woman lead, how many women speaking as secondary characters, how many women below the line [crew members]. If you hit points like these, you get the stamp.

The next one is a protégé programme. We found in our research there's an issue with mid-career women. For mid-career women who have done a film at a film festival, it takes seven years to do the next film, as compared to 70 per cent of men who've had films in festivals and their next film in two years. And why is that? It's because of the support from the top. How do you get a team of people to be your cheerleaders, who will call studios for you and say, 'You should hire this woman,' or 'Please take a look at this woman'? There are so many more women directing and doing great stuff who are just not given the opportunity. That's what our protégé programme is about.

Whether it is pay, promotion or opportunity, women can still find themselves being treated differently in workplaces across the world. In looking at three sectors – sport, special forces, and Hollywood – we see how great these disparities can be. But just because the gaps are huge (or, in Seema Rao's case, no women are allowed to participate in India's elite special force units) it doesn't mean perceptions can't be challenged or gaps closed. It could take a generation or more for female footballers to earn anywhere near their male counterparts' pay – but other sports, such as tennis where the top Grand Slam tournaments have offered equal prize money to male and female champions for over a decade, can show the way. And, with committed industry professionals in Hollywood determined to take structured action to address inequality, there is a blueprint for the film industry to take the next step in levelling the playing field.

DR SEEMA RAO
Real-life Wonder Woman

Dr Seema Rao is a combat training instructor who has spent nearly two decades training Indian special forces. An excellent markswoman, she is a pioneer in developing close-quarters battle techniques. As well as being a doctor of medicine, she is a seventh-degree black-belt holder in military martial arts, a trained firefighter, a scuba diver, an HMI medallist in rock-climbing and a Mrs India World pageant finalist. Rao is a co-author of the training manual Encyclopedia of Close Combat Ops and has published the first Indian book on terrorism, A Comprehensive Analysis of World Terrorism. Her other works, including Commando Manual of Unarmed Combat, are currently held for use by agencies such as the FBI.

66 It all started because I was born in a patriotic family. My father was a freedom fighter involved in the struggle against the Portuguese. Then, as I grew up, I had certain issues. I was quiet and I was bullied at school. However, I had a strong desire to change who I was. I wanted to be somebody in control of my situation, not controlled by the situation. I didn't know how to make that happen. I think my vocation, as commander of the forces, is unusual. But if I look at the kind of person I was, I was not made for that. But the fire within me was a desperate need to change, to make myself strong.

I became an expert in unarmed combat, then went on to shooting. I am a sharp shooter, and my husband and I started teaching forces shooting. Basically, I specialise in close-quarters battle, which is fighting with the enemy at about twenty yards – unarmed combat, team-on-team tactics, shooting, the works. We have been the pioneers of an innovative shooting method, which has proved quite useful to the forces. We call it the Rao Reflex Shooting Method.

I think women should do well in combat, because it needs a lot of mental strength. Physical strength can be built. Sometimes when I grapple with my trainees, they are half my age and twice my weight, but I know exactly how to bring them down. Women do very well because they work with their heart and their soul and in a different fashion from men. When it comes to shooting, women shoot very naturally.

I am called often to give motivational talks to colleges, to young girls of between fifteen and twenty. I speak to them about my life and how I went about it.

I tell them you have to have a passion for what you want to do in life. The second thing is that they must also understand they will be faced with misfortune and the decisions they take will determine whether they make it or not. The third thing I tell them is that failure is a part of everybody. But failure can either shine a light on your goals or inhibit you. You have to challenge it.

I also tell them to express themselves. Often people are afraid to do this. They are afraid of ridicule. But I tell them that expression is very important, because through it something magical can happen. So, be fearless in your expression, be fearless in your mind. Expect the obstacle ahead but challenge yourself and overcome it.

I tell them to keep their minds open. Sometimes, if you're faced with an obstacle, you only see one way out of it, but there are different ways to overcome an obstacle. **"**

MARIA BELLO
Actor

Actress, producer and campaigner, Maria Bello has long been in the vanguard of Hollywood's feminist movement. From E.R. *to* Coyote Ugly *via* A History of Violence, *her portrayal of strong female characters is true to the woman herself. An advocate of equal opportunities in film and television, and campaigner against sexual harassment, Bello's arguments have found a new home in the #MeToo movement.*

❝ I was never an ingénue. At twenty-eight, I arrived in Los Angeles from New York City with my black army boots, which I always wore, and my fuck-you attitude. And it worked for me because I was different and I did take ownership of myself. I never forgot where I came from and I still don't. Of course I can have polite conversation, but I'll never throw out the girl from Philly. I'm not interested in losing my history, my past, which has helped me become what I am.

When I'm looking at a script, the page has to activate me emotionally in my gut, sexually, intellectually. I would say the 'sexy' roles I've done have been very complex characters. When I look at my award-winning roles – in *The Cooler* and *A History of Violence* – yes, there was nudity, there was sex, but they were deep wells of women and I'm proud of that. I don't believe it's one or the other.

The idea of a sixty-year-old man and the wife or the girlfriend being thirty years old, I can't even look at those scripts any more. Just recently I was offered a movie playing the girlfriend of a guy who's seventy, just the girl on the side. I said no. It didn't interest me. I have my own opportunities in my age range. The big reason, I think, that I continue to work and get really exciting roles is because I don't try to look twenty. I look my age. I look good for my age, but I'm my age, too.

When women feel the need to compete by doing things to their faces and bodies so that they don't look real, then complain about not getting roles, it's like they're fishing in the wrong pond.

When you take ownership of yourself, there's more possibility in our business. In Europe there is much more room for women as they age. When I look at Helen Mirren, when I look at Isabelle Huppert, when I look at Sarah Lancashire, they're real role models for me getting older. I think we all need role models, mentors, people we can look up to and say, 'I wanna be that.' Not meaning 'I wanna be you', but 'I wanna be as self-possessed as you are.' You look at Jane Fonda and the work she's done as an actress, how gorgeous and sexy she is, and that is because she has complete ownership of herself. If I could wish for anything for anyone, it would be that, including for myself.

I think women are the keepers of stories and we need to be, because without our stories there's nothing but life pages. And it takes our strength to carry that pain and that burden, yet I think it's the only way forward. **"**

Antisocial Media

Every advance in communication – from the printing press to the telephone to television – has led to the democratisation of ideas. Each has – eventually – led to women gaining a bigger voice, finding places and media to express opinions, open up discussion and raise issues.

However, in some cultures those technologies have been used to suppress freedom, spread propaganda and take away rights. We should be proud that that has not happened in the UK or, arguably, in any Western democracy with any of the traditional technologies. But there is an exception to the rule that new technologies always give women a greater voice in a democracy. That is online and, specifically, social media.

Far from being a place where women can feel free to express themselves, social media too often becomes somewhere that the kind of abuse of women we thought we were eradicating has space to thrive. Responses to women's opinions are too often answered with the most graphic threats of rape, violence and even murder.

Twitter gives these instructions: 'Find a bunch of things you love. And then find people to follow. That's all you need to do to see and talk about what is happening.' But that is not the experience of thousands of women, who hoped that would be true. Women who would appreciate a platform like that for the discussion of ideas. Too often it seems that some Twitter users 'find a bunch of things they hate. And then find people to hate. Then tell them how much they hate them. And why.'

Amnesty International recently researched the problem and produced a report: 'Toxic Twitter – A Toxic Place for Women'. They polled women in eight different countries on their online experience and a quarter said they had experienced abuse, often from complete strangers. A quarter of those threats were of physical or sexual violence. Well over half expressed general misogyny.

I was surprised by the findings. I was surprised the numbers were so low.

As a female politician, with female colleagues from across the political spectrum, I don't know of a single one who hasn't been insulted, threatened, abused, mocked or dismissed. Not one whose motives haven't been questioned, whose appearance hasn't been derided and who hasn't been told multiple, multiple times that their voice is not welcome in the public debate. Not one who hasn't been subject to vile imagery and coarse, expletive-laden language.

For my own part, the regular misogyny is often spiced with a good dose of homophobia. There seems to be a fairly significant number of men, none of whom are keen to publish their actual names, who have put serious thought into what needs to be 'done' to me to make me change my sexuality.

When I speak to newly elected members or new hires who are coming to work for the Scottish Conservatives, I give them all the same pep-talk on how to gauge their own social media responses, even in the face of extreme provocation. 'Don't say anything online that you wouldn't say to a man a foot taller than you, two foot wider than you, pissed, and waving a broken glass around in a pub.' As a rule of thumb, I still think that holds.

But it's not just politicians for whom social media can be a daily trial. Women who are not in the public eye are targeted too. Their tormentor often starts with gender, but goes on to attack every aspect of their target from sexual orientation to race, ethnicity and even disability. Women's rights activist Laura Bates started the Everyday Sexism Project, in which people can use the hashtag to highlight casual sexism. From the start she received up to 200 abusive online messages each day. As her profile grew the abuse spread. She said: 'They often spike if I've been in the media. You could be sitting at home in your living room, outside working hours, and suddenly someone sends you a graphic rape threat, right into the palm of your hand.'

Amnesty found that around 3.5 per cent of tweets contain outright abuse. Which sounds small, but when you take into account that 500 million tweets are sent every day worldwide, that is 17 million abusive tweets a day, every day – over half a billion a month. When your phone starts buzzing with even a few dozen, alerts go off again and again as others share and 'like' the abuse. It doesn't take much to feel hunted.

The result is that women's voices are silenced. The medium becomes a tool for nothing more than cute dog pictures or cat GIFs, or the hounding is such that people choose simply to leave.

It's an issue that even Twitter recognises. Former CEO Dick Costolo admits, 'We suck at dealing with abuse and trolls on the platform and we've sucked at it for years. We lose core user after core user by not addressing simple trolling issues that they face every day. I'm frankly ashamed of how poorly we've dealt with this issue during my tenure as CEO. It's absurd. There's no excuse for it.'

His successor, Jack Dorsey, says the team have tried to tackle the problem, but were swamped: 'We see voices silenced on Twitter every day. We've been working to counteract this for the past two years. We prioritised it in 2016. We updated our policies and increased the size of our teams. It wasn't enough.' New efforts by Dorsey and his team to counteract the negativity of the discussion on Twitter are expected to be announced this year.

If Twitter and other online platforms were just a fad, then perhaps women could walk away and wait until they became merely a circle-jerk of the abusive running out of targets and were eventually closed down. But we can't. As the United Nations has acknowledged, this is a matter of human rights.

Social-media platforms are where a lot of political debate now happens. Many younger voters don't want to be told things curated and edited by traditional outlets: they want to be able to discuss them. Social-media platforms are where that debate happens. As US journalist Imani Gandy told Amnesty: 'Twitter has become the new public square. I've found Twitter to be a really good platform for people who normally don't have much of a say in the political process.'

If Twitter is the new public square for political debate – where people not normally engaged in politics engage – then it is not simply ironic that a hundred years since some women were enfranchised in Britain they are being chased out of that public square. It is a disgrace that undermines our democracy. The UN has recognised this, saying that online abuse can 'chill and disrupt the online participation of women journalists, activists, human-rights defenders, artists and other public figures and private persons'.

The more contentious the issue, the more women's voices are likely to be shouted down and the stronger the voice, the greater the abuse. As journalist Nosheen Iqbal told Amnesty: 'Expressing an opinion or a strong opinion will get you roasted online. The most memorable is when someone has a large following and all the followers jump in. You just don't expect it – you shouldn't expect it. Attitudes to women are heinous online.'

The abuse of women is even used to target men. The *Times Literary Supplement* editor, Stig Abell, received tweets from a troll who graphically threatened to rape his wife in vengeance for his opinions. The aggressor started commenting that he was outside the couple's house and talked about which lights were on. Twitter's initial response was to do nothing – claiming the content didn't breach their rules. Eventually they acted, after strong pushback from users.

It seems absurd that the protections people enjoy offline do not carry in practice into the online space. Threatening to assault, rape or murder a woman in the street is a crime. Yet emboldened by anonymity, many men think they can get away with it online. And that anonymity can make the threat even more chilling for the victim. 'Doxing' – publishing women's home addresses and personal details online against their will – adds a frightening, real-world threat to internet abuse.

In my own case, I've had pictures I didn't know were being taken of me posted online in real time, alerting people to which shop or pub I was in, and details of the train I was on published to a website dedicated to documenting politicians' whereabouts.

I've changed my own social-media use. After several attempted breaches of security of my personal Facebook account, when I was a by-election candidate, I came off the platform completely. My office now runs a vanilla page on my behalf. While on Twitter, what started as a puckish and irreverent skip through my daily musings, political work, interaction on the topic of the day, jokes with journalists and recommendations of good articles to read has changed completely. No longer is Twitter much of an interactive experience: my account is far more set to 'transmit' than 'receive'. Instead of the personal or quirky, it looks very much like any other politician's page: pictures of people campaigning on the doorstep, pre-prepared graphics from the party put out to highlight whichever policy we're promoting that day, and snaps of me meeting with charities, businesses or groups of schoolchildren at the Scottish Parliament. Over the years, I've been fortunate enough to win awards – in Scotland and at UK level – for social-media use. I doubt there will be any more. I am simply tired of wading through the mire of people who have no wish to engage in the substance of debate, but just want to call me a string of four-letter words. Until that changes, I'm done. And the mute button is my friend.

It's a response echoed by Labour's shadow home secretary, Diane Abbott. 'The abuse that I get online does limit my freedom of expression. I now spend much less time on Twitter than I used to because the abuse is so terrible.'

This is not just a matter of women's rights. It is also a question of freedom of expression and democracy. We have fought too hard, for too long, and made too much progress to allow new technology to revive old evils. In the US, the National Network to End Domestic Violence reported that 97 per cent of their programmes said that technology was used as a tool of abuse.

In the civil war in the Democratic Republic of Congo, rape is used as a weapon. Occasionally this is reported on our television screens and we warm ourselves with the assurance that things like that could not happen here because of our values. Yet in our democracy – and across the democratic world – the threat of rape is used online as a weapon against women.

There is now a consensus that we should continue the fight to make sure we have more women politicians, journalists, and women in the higher echelons of business, academia and all aspects of public life. There is a consensus for equality of pay and esteem. But however successful those efforts may be, they will be of little use if those same women can be silenced by anonymous threats of violence – if women strive to be seen but are not allowed to be heard. If these threats were as regularly made in licensed premises as they are online, those venues hosting such attacks would be closed down.

New technologies that should free people are too often used to air old bigotry and violence, to oppress and silence women. There needs to be more done online not just to protect our data but to protect our safety and dignity.

The printing press, the telephone and television: if someone printed rape threats, they would be jailed, similarly, if they made them over the telephone; regulation means no television channel is free to air the same. Yet in our latest and perhaps greatest technological advance, the internet, such threats are not just allowed to go unpunished but for many women they are the common currency of their lives online. Digital communication is not a hobby but a vital part of our national conversation.

Women across the country are proud to have marched to 'reclaim the night' so that others do not fear being attacked if they walk the streets after dark. We are in danger of allowing online platforms like Twitter to become the darkest of street corners where women fear to tread.

The BBC's Laura Kuenssberg is directly affected by online abuse. As its political editor, social media is an essential tool of her job. With at least three-quarters of a million followers to her Twitter account, it is a huge platform from which she can communicate the stories of the day. She has frequently been a target, a magnet for sexist and bullying comments. Around the last general election, the online threats to her became so great that her employer insisted she was issued with a bodyguard to accompany her as she toured the country covering the various campaigns.

66 *Social media is an important place because lots of the audience are there. Twitter's important, but it's not the real world. Lots of people follow and lots are probably bots, so in terms of counting it as an audience, you've got to be pretty careful about what it is and what it's not. That said, it's obviously a big platform so we have to be there.*

It's like a megaphone for both positive and negative. When something amazing happens – Andy Murray wins Wimbledon – there's huge love and it's a massively positive place. It's also a very dark place. People would never say to you in the street what they say about you online. For a long time, there's been a particularly virulent, unpleasant strain of stuff directed at me.

In previous jobs I used Twitter for interacting with people and saying, 'I'm about to ask questions of this person in an interview. What are you interested in?' or 'We're doing a piece about GDP. Are you a business in Manchester and do you want to chat?' I used it as an open forum. Now, there's just too much bile.

If I ask an open question on Twitter, the stuff I get back! If I click on the @ button, too much of it is vile, and sometimes violent, so I just don't look at it. I know people take different approaches and some colleagues make a point of retweeting the horrible stuff or blocking. I don't look because I sense that that's what people want. I just don't respond.

I care most about attacks that we are biased. The reason we exist and the reason that the public pays for us, is because we have higher standards than other people. We're there on behalf of nobody other than the people who are paying our wages. You get stuff that's straight down the line. It's impartial, and that's what I care about most. If people go after that, it really, really winds me up.

Abuse of women is not a new phenomenon. But the technologies that have allowed persistent targeting have developed in a relatively short period. Tech entrepreneur Baroness Lane Fox believes the current online-abuse issue will be resolved – and that it says more about those who feel it is acceptable to target women than about the platforms themselves. Lane Fox says she agreed to join the board of Twitter in part to 'try and keep them honest'. She wants to see more women making decisions in tech so that the differing experiences of men and women are given proper attention.

The World Economic Forum has done studies on the absence of women's voices on social-media platforms: they're being quietened because of the abuse. If women in public office aren't out there in public, or don't want to run for public office, you quickly end up in a very bad place.

One of the reasons I wanted to be on the board of Twitter is because I love the platform. I can see its value. I don't think I'm being naïve, but I feel quite optimistic because this is still so new. It doesn't feel new if you've been abused, if you've had death or rape threats – and I'm not suggesting for one minute that that isn't extremely serious – but, if you look at the genesis of our technology, then I think it's new.

Twitter is just ten years old. Facebook is marginally older, and I think that they would say that they got some things wrong. They didn't design it with this as an intended consequence.

I think Jack Dorsey, the founder of Twitter, has a real grip and has signalled his intention to have a public conversation about the public health of the platform. There's a good thought at the heart of it: how do you measure whether we're contributing to a net gain or net negative to conversation, to civility, to how people treat each other?

When these guys move – a bit like government – they have power to move at scale and speed. So I think you will see some changes coming up in the next year that will be good, both about authenticity, danger tweets, and so on. But, more importantly, perhaps, the general philosophy behind the platform, that we must just let people say whatever they like, has dramatically changed. Clearly, what's happened with Facebook and the data will make for more change. We will look back upon all of this, maybe in a couple of years, and think, Whoa, that was bad, but thank God we worked through it.

These are still only technologies. Human beings run the platforms and they are not evil monsters trying to destroy the world.

I'm not a tech apologist at all for these guys, but from what I know about Twitter I feel quite optimistic that there will be another kind of Twitter within the next two to three years.

It's not just about the technologies that are currently available but also the next big thing. Melinda Gates believes women aren't benefited by tech, and in some cases are actively inhibited by it, because they are not represented at the development stage. Gates studied computer science in the 1980s and joined Microsoft on graduation. She says the tech sector is a fantastic place to work, with more and more companies needing technologists, but an ever-lower proportion of female technologists are graduating. If women are to have a positive experience from new advances, Gates believes they must shape them as they develop.

When I was in college 37 per cent of computer-science grads were women; we're down now to 18 per cent. We literally thought we were on the rise – at the same time as medicine was on the rise. It just doesn't make sense that we've had this dip. And it means that as tech is changing the world, women's voices and ideas are missing.

When I think about what is going to happen with AI, Artificial Intelligence – to not have women at that table will have such broad implications for society. That really makes me concerned. That's why I'm using my voice to try and put some investments down. How do we open up those pathways to get more girls and women to go into tech?

If you don't have women at the table, you won't have an equal view of society. We will bias AI in favour of – and this is a gross generalisation – a Caucasian guy in a hoodie. Unless you have diverse points of view around the table from people of different skin colours and different genders you're not going to represent all people and you'll bias the system. Even in health, you'll bias it. We're finally un-biasing health research: we used to think a woman's body was just a riff of a man's body in terms of how it worked biologically. We're learning that medicines work differently in women's bodies than they do in men's because we have women at the table, saying, 'Hey, we gotta have more women in the trials for these things.' It's really, really important.

Asked how she would get more women to choose a career in the science, engineering and tech sectors, Melinda Gates is firm in her belief that we have to change the way in which we educate our young people:

I would create more pathways for girls. I would have more role models speaking out and women who look very different from one another, just like we do for men. Men don't look up and see one or two types of men, they look up and three dozen different types of men are leading the world. Our female role models need to look very different from one another so girls will think, Well, I don't look like her . . . but I kinda look like her. I wanna be like that one.

But we also have to create all these pathways in for girls, so we have to de-bias what I call the Computer Science 101 course.

Every computer-science intro course at college should become popular because it's fun to go into and it's interesting to girls and boys. Today that CS 101 class goes towards the geeky math boys. When you de-bias that class and you make it about real world problems, many more girls flood into it.

How do we open up those pathways to get more girls and women to want to go into tech?

While, clearly, there is a concerted attempt to address the inequities ingrained in tech – in terms of female strategic direction and women's participation rates as users – one woman is on a mission to write women back into the narrative. The broadcaster Sandi Toksvig is asking thousands of women to take responsibility for a female contributor to human history, who is not included in the online canon, and to create a place for her in the digital archives.

One of my big projects that I'm working on at the moment is about Wikipedia.

Wikipedia is the largest access information site in the world in terms of people wanting to look up history or biographies. Currently, the information online is 91 per cent male and 9 per cent female.

If you want to find a biography of an amazing woman, you might think she didn't exist or she had nothing to do with the subject you're looking up because you won't find her on Wikipedia.

History, at the moment, literally needs to be rewritten or women will be written out of it. There are roughly 350,000 editors of Wikipedia – it's an entirely democratic encyclopaedia to which anyone can contribute. Ninety per cent of the contributors are male, nine per cent are female, and one per cent refuse to give their identity. And that is almost exactly the same as the content.

In 2014, one of the contributors to the list of Great American Novels took out all the women and placed them in a separate Great Women Novelists list. But they didn't do the same for Great Male Novelists. It was just the Great American Novel, but they were all written by men.

I've currently got a list of 4,000 great female scientists who are not on Wikipedia and need to be inputted.

I'm writing a show which is a history of the world according to women. I will do it in very big venues – 2,500 people – and I will get every person in the audience to commit to looking after one woman to make sure she's on Wikipedia.

It's a huge project and it must be done.

The last huge piece of writing done over a long period of time by a large group of people, was the Bible, and women speak in the Bible one per cent of the time. Let's not have it happen again. Let's not be written out of history. That is what's happening today.

There is nothing inevitable about the sidelining of women from digital forums or social-media coffee houses, and a number of committed campaigners and tech entrepreneurs are working hard to level the playing field. Just as women have taken it upon themselves to demand physical safety and respect with 'Reclaim the Night', now they are acting to reclaim the digital streets.

MELINDA GATES
**Philanthropist, Bill and
Melinda Gates Foundation**

*When computer scientist Melinda French joined the Microsoft
Corporation in 1987, she could not have predicted where life would
take her. Following her marriage to Bill Gates in 1994, she and her
husband set up what would become the Bill and Melinda Gates
Foundation. Today, their work has improved the life chances of millions
of people worldwide. Melinda is a passionate advocate of female
education and access to contraception in some of the world's most
challenging countries. Together – whether fighting malaria or encouraging more women into tech – the Gates continue to harness their
immense wealth for good.*

66 At high school, I had a very enlightened math teacher who
convinced the principals to get us girls some computers. It
was serendipitous that she did that. I was a good math
student, and she said, 'If you want to program, we could learn
programs.' She taught us courage. She let the girls get ahead of
her because she was also learning how to program. Because of
that, I fell in love with it. I always loved puzzles, games and
math.

After I graduated I had several job offers but the reason I
chose Microsoft – definitely not for the starting salary I'll tell
you that – was that they were changing the world and they
knew it. They were on the cusp of something. The company

had fewer than 1,700 employees but they knew they were changing the world and I wanted to be part of that. It was so exciting. Sometimes we were having to wait for the hardware and catch up with the ideas we had for the software. We had big plans. And it was fun.

Before Bill and I got married, we decided the resources that had been amassed from Microsoft would go back via a foundation to the world. For me, it really comes back to my family and where I went to high school. I'm Catholic, and I went to a school run by Ursuline nuns. Their motto was 'Serviam', meaning 'I will serve'. With the foundation, it just made sense to me to go back to the values of 'I will serve' and to think about what would I want if my family and I were poor. What could help us lift ourselves? It's all about dignity. You want to lift yourself out of poverty.

When we started to look at the problems of the world, we found that a mother or father might be dealing with five bouts of malaria in their family each year, or that they couldn't get basic vaccines so their child had measles. They couldn't feed their kids. It made sense for us to go into global health. So we researched and systematically figured out the places that a foundation could change things at scale for people.

Then we realised it had to be done in a culturally sensitive way. Years ago, when we were first coming into this global health work, President Carter said to me, 'What you have to know, Melinda, is that whatever programme you're involved in, the community has to take it up and think it's theirs from the get-go. That's if you want lasting change. If they don't think it's theirs, you won't get real ownership of it. Then, when you leave or your partner leaves, it doesn't sustain. But if it's their work, they believe in it, they have the same values, and you're teaching them. They'll sustain the work and carry on.' **"**

LAURA KUENSSBERG
Political editor, BBC News

Laura Kuenssberg, political editor for BBC News, studied history at the University of Edinburgh, followed by journalism at Georgetown University in the United States. She has worked for both of the main television networks in the UK, serving first as chief political correspondent for the BBC, then as business editor at ITV before she took up her current post.

" I remember during the 2010 election looking one way in Downing Street and it was all blokes, and looking the other and it was all blokes.

Basically, the higher you go, the lonelier it is in terms of being the only woman. By virtue of that, you notice it a lot less when you're starting out, but it becomes more profound.

I don't think being a woman has ever stopped me doing anything, but it's hard to persuade people to take you seriously. The old adage that you have to be better is absolutely true, and some people do dismiss you, no question.

But you can use the fact that you may be the only woman to your advantage. In an industry that's very competitive, everybody's looking for a way to stand out. If you're in a press

141

conference and you're the only female reporter, it's possible you'll be called, because it looks different.

Politics is so tribal. There are two ways of doing it. Some politicians reach out and want all sorts of different people in their team. Others, in a very tough, bruising game, surround themselves with people like them. In my experience, the politicians who choose to surround themselves with people like them are irritated when you come in, a generation younger, a different gender, and ask them difficult questions. They find it more difficult to deal with than if somebody of their gender and generation asks the same questions. I have definitely found that, from both major political parties. Some people have remarked, 'You really wind him up more than the others,' and I have reflected on it and thought, Yeah, that's probably right.

It's a huge privilege, a huge honour, to do this job, and carries with it a huge responsibility. I feel that responsibility very keenly. Not long after I got the job, the Chinese president was here and I asked him a really tough question about human rights. It was really important to do that as I am doing the job on behalf of the BBC.

As a woman, I also felt a different type of pressure. Once I've done this job, there'll be one less reason for women to say, 'Oh, I couldn't do it.' I've set an example, particularly for younger women: I have a public profile as being serious, an expert and for finding things out. I'm not there because I've got great hair. I am proud that I'm the first woman to do my job and the youngest person to have done it. **"**

7

Activism

We weren't a family who marched, or wrote to our MP, or even sounded the car horn when we passed a picket line. We were a family who worked hard, paid our taxes, read the daily newspaper (sports pages first), had the TV news on in the background while Mum was cooking tea, and who tutted disapproval if the government did something we disagreed with.

Activism didn't exist. There was only doing your bit or helping out. I remember holding the dog while Mum trailed us round the village posting charity envelopes through doors, raising money for Christian Aid, Scottish Spastics (now Scope), the Brittle Bone Society and several others, many times a year, every year. Fundraising for school or church charities was an important business and required thought and application. And our actions at home were judged on a much wider spectrum – fail to finish your tea and the threat to send your week's food to starving children in Ethiopia, Biafra or wherever the Blue

Peter Appeal was raising funds for was made with such force you believed it. Fail to finish your veg for a second time in a week, and the threat level rose: you'd be swapped with a child from such a country who *would* appreciate the food placed in front of them. More than one night I went to bed fearful that I'd soon be on a plane to sub-Saharan Africa.

Doing what was right was important. On the run-up to every election, my parents' polling cards were placed on the mantelpiece as a reminder. You cast your vote in person – no postal applications in our house – and in our younger years, my sister and I were encouraged to walk with Mum to the local primary school to help her do her democratic duty (my dad would drive home from work via the polling station). No votes were ever missed.

Elections had value. We knew that: after my sister and I had been dispatched to bed, my parents would stay up through the night to watch the results come in. Occasionally, we would be wakened by a shout in the wee small hours if something of note had occurred. I distinctly remember the 1992 UK general election. I would have been thirteen and it took place during the Easter holidays. After voting, we had gone away for a long weekend to a log cabin/bunkhouse/chalet affair in Perthshire. The walls were very thin.

All the polls had pointed to a change of government, from Conservative to Labour. The Labour leader, Neil Kinnock, had already held a victory rally ahead of polling day. Turnout was huge and – against predictions – John Major was returned as prime minister. I awoke to my bunk bed shaking as my father jumped to his feet next door exclaiming at the surprise result.

Such was its relevance, he even blundered through to explain to his grumpy teenage children what had just taken place. We were less than thrilled at the interruption. However, as he had semi-seriously threatened to emigrate with the whole family in tow if Neil Kinnock triumphed (he was not a fan), our sleeplessness was confined to a few minutes. At least we wouldn't be leaving home.

But something must have stuck. I remember following the next year's American presidential election intently. And thereafter staying up late to watch successive State of the Union addresses from President Clinton who, at the time, I considered the best orator on the world stage. With my Martin Luther King poster on my bedroom wall, with passages of his 'I Have a Dream' speech superimposed over the great man's head, I thought America was entering a new golden age of politics.

My own entry into electoral engagement occurred in 1997, my first year at university. At eighteen I took my electoral commitments so seriously that I decided I would travel home and back to vote in the parliamentary seat I'd grown up in, rather than the one in which my student flat was located. I had a better knowledge of the candidates and felt my vote mattered more there. One of the university's student unions had applied for a special licence so it could keep the bar open and show the results programme through the night. One of my friends had got tickets for us all. It wasn't until I arrived that they told me the union had been hired by the university's Labour Club. I would be the only Tory in a room of 250 lefty students baying for the fall of the UK government after eighteen years at the helm. To say it was character-building is an understatement.

Not only did the Conservatives get thoroughly routed, but they lost every single MP in the whole of Scotland. Every time a Scottish seat was announced, another cheer went up and I ordered another double vodka. It was a long trudge home the following morning.

My non-activism continued after university. As a student, I'd never joined the university Conservative Club as it was full of people who were odd, earnest, English and deeply uncool. As a journalist, I'd been warned early on by a local MSP that if I was ever considering politics, I shouldn't join a party – just resolve to be the best, most even-handed broadcaster I could be. My professional accomplishments would be enough to recommend me if I ever chose to swap sides of the microphone.

It was advice that I took to heart. If anything, I was probably tougher on my own side. During the 2005 leadership election for the UK Conservative Party, the BBC radio programme I presented interviewed all five of the long-listed candidates. While I was questioning the former foreign secretary, Sir Malcolm Rifkind, down the line from London, he got up and stormed out of the interview halfway through. Apparently he objected to being asked whether he and another contender – Kenneth Clarke – having served as ministers throughout the entire Thatcher administration several decades past, might be considered 'dinosaurs from a bygone age'.

I was serious about my work as a journalist. I wanted not just to be impartial but to be seen to be impartial. However, there was one issue I felt strongly enough about to break BBC rules and take a political stand. It was also the first time I marched.

The national debate about committing troops to a second Gulf War was fierce. Parliamentary clashes, UN motions and intelligence dossiers on the chemical and biological weapons capability of the Iraq regime – and Saddam Hussein's willingness to deploy such against his own people – dominated the news headlines night after night. It was a textbook example of a 'controversial area of policy' and the BBC's guidelines about news staff taking a stand on such issues are crystal-clear:

> Presenters, reporters and editorial people in news, current affairs, topical and consumer programmes should not normally associate themselves with any campaigning body, particularly if it backs one viewpoint in a controversial area of policy . . . Political activity by individuals, including on-air talent on long-term contracts, must not compromise the BBC's impartiality or undermine public confidence in the BBC. Judgements about what is acceptable will reflect individual circumstances, including the type of activity and the nature of the individual's BBC role. Political activity or taking a public position on an issue of public policy, political or industrial controversy, or any other 'controversial subject' is likely to be incompatible with some BBC roles, especially in news, current affairs and, sometimes, in general factual programmes.

Two big marches were due to take place against Britain committing troops to an invasion force, one in London, the other in Glasgow, where I lived and worked. I had spent years dreaming of working for BBC News and, within six months of finally getting a job with the Corporation, I was considering jeopardising it all to become a face in a – large – crowd that I did not think for one second would actually stay the government's hand. Also, my reasons for marching were not the same as everyone else's. Many were there because they believed military action – all military action – was wrong. That was not me. I have always been of the some-peace-*is*-worth-fighting-for school of thought. And my time in Kosovo just a couple of years before had reinforced in me the belief that UK armed forces could be a force for good in the world – I'd seen it with my own eyes.

No, I was marching to try to keep the government honest. Tony Blair was keen to have UN backing for any military action that Britain undertook in Iraq. But he knew it was highly unlikely that an explicit resolution for military action would pass. The UK government therefore argued that a previous resolution gave scope for action by force. I thought it was sophistry of the highest order to argue that an endorsement had already been given, when ministers knew that if they sought such an endorsement they would not receive it.

My own personal conflict was heightened by the fact that I'd recently sorted out the leave-and-shift dispensation I required from the BBC to join the reserve forces and had put in my application just a few weeks before. My interview for entry was within the month and, believing in the chain of command, I would not refuse to serve if I was required to. Therefore I was marching against a conflict that hadn't started, in which I could be called to participate. If I was, I had resolved to go so no one else would have to take my place.

I was joined by another new hire at the BBC, now a senior

correspondent, who was as nervous as I was about breaking impartiality and possibly getting censured or sacked. Of course, as a politician, I've attended dozens of marches and rallies. I've tabled motions and started petitions, set up campaign groups, written letters and made speeches in support of others trying to change some element of law or practice. As a member of a (non-affiliated) trade union for a decade, I've stood on picket lines and I've badgered any number of housing associations, council departments or government agencies to act on specific issues affecting constituents.

As a legislator, I've been subject to intense lobbying. The wellspring of online campaigning sites means people concerned about an issue don't need to draft correspondence: they can simply enter their postcode, click a button, and a campaign letter will be sent to their local MP or MSP. Representatives receive hundreds of such emails a week. I endeavour to respond to all – and always have a wee chuckle if, as has happened, someone comes back to complain they got exactly the same response as their mate, who dispatched exactly the same pro-forma email on the same subject.

But the advent of such campaign tools hasn't dimmed enthusiasm for more traditional campaigning methods. Rallies and marches, speeches and placards look set to be part of our body politic for some time, alongside consumer activism – voting with your wallet – and a recent upswing in shareholder activism too. Social media can bring those with more niche concerns – and therefore more likely to be geographically spread – into instant contact, while campaign tools and results are much easier to share. The public forum has never seemed so vibrant, or groups of people fighting for their cause more engaged. As long as activism does not spill over into abuse – in person or online – public debate is in a healthy state. But, as there is no optimum and all countries strive for better, there are still mountains to climb and conquer and changes to fight for.

From the suffragettes and suffragists of a century ago until now, women have always been at the heart of political activism, which can take many forms. Each of the women detailed below has decided to take on a government, political system, global industry, or empower the next generation of women. They all want voices that have been marginalised or ignored brought into the mainstream. They should inspire all of us to believe that change is possible, and we can help create it.

As the daughter of Robert F. Kennedy, Kerry Kennedy grew up with activists in and out of her home from early childhood. The human rights organisation she set up in her father's name doesn't just lobby governments and challenge injustice through the courts, it also runs an enormous schools programme, giving the next generation the basic tools to assert their rights and effect change. Kennedy believes that it is a moral imperative to instruct young people on activism. The organisation runs a human rights education programme that reaches 1.2 million children around the world each year.

❝ *We don't teach a course, we say to teachers, 'What are you teaching?' and then we create lesson commands for that particular country around the things they are already teaching.*

For example, kids that are twelve years old have to take language art – when I was a kid it was called English, but now it's called language art. They have to learn poetry. That's their first lesson. We give them two or three articles about the manu-facturing of chocolate. Seventy per cent of the chocolate consumed in the UK is made by children in slavery or child labour.

That comes as a shock to most students. They can't believe their chocolate is made by children in slavery. They have to write a poem . . . from the perspective of the child in slave labour in the chocolate industry. They're learning textual analysis, social and emotional empathy and poetry – they have to write it in iambic pentameter.

Then, a few weeks later, they have to do expository writing. We give them the same articles, and we give them the name and address of Mars or Hersheys – Cadbury's in the UK – and they have to write a letter to the CEO of that company saying, 'Here's the problem,' and 'What are you doing to fix it?'

So they're learning again: textual analysis, social and emotional learning. They are translating something that is an emotional issue into an advocacy piece. And then they're learning how to write a business letter – where does the stamp go? Return address, etc. These are facts they need to learn to get to graduate school.

Finally, we give them a 5 x 8-inch index card. They have to consolidate their thoughts and write the problem in one sentence. Then they tape a piece of Fairtrade chocolate to the card and say, 'This is the solution: Fairtrade chocolate.' On Hallowe'en, whenever someone gives them a piece of chocolate, they do reverse trick-or-treat. They say, 'Thank you very much. Can I give you this card?'

And through that process they learn about the issue, they learn how to make a difference and they create change. And that's a very empowering set of things for them to do. It makes them feel alive -- there aren't just problems in the world, there are solutions, and I can be part of creating change.

The broadcaster Sandy Toksvig co-founded the Women's Equality Party in the UK to get more women into politics, a fairer deal across the sexes and for more women to be heard. She's working hard to support women to become political activists, candidates and spokespeople on women's issues. One of the dedicated goals of the WEP is breaking down barriers that stop more women entering mainstream politics.

What you have to look at is why women are not activists. Quite often it is difficult for them. We are the very first party – as far as I know in the world – that offers free childcare for anyone who would like to stand for it. We have a special fund and we fundraise for the purpose. If you decide to become a candidate for our party, and you have children, we will pay for the children to be looked after so you can come out, doorstep and leaflet.

And what happened is that we released women to come to hustings, to address a conference. We are training women to do public speaking, to become more confident, to have a view.

We had an amazing moment at conference. Fifteen hundred people turned up at our first and I announced that we were going to have a three-hour session where anyone could come up and have the microphone. If they had something to say and felt that their voice wasn't being heard, this was the moment.

And people were queuing up to speak and sometimes they just wanted to say, 'I'm Ethel, I'm eighty-five, and have never been to a political gathering before. I've been waiting my whole life for this to happen.' Just wonderful stuff.

And I said, 'If you're scared to come up, I'll just come up with you because I'm not scared of anything.' So this young girl was absolutely shaking – she was about nineteen – and I said, 'If nothing else, just get up and say your name. Then you've spoken to conference and your voice has been heard.'

I put my arm around her and she spoke and said her name, and why she'd come, and a couple of things about why it was important to her. And she got such a cheer – the crowd was fantastic.

About three-quarters of an hour later I've got my arm round another young person, taking her up on stage, and there's a tap

on my shoulder. It's the first girl, and she says, 'I'll take her up.'
That was one of the most empowering things that's ever
happened to me.

Those are people who felt politics was nothing to do with them,
who were shouted down. That was great.

The actress Maria Bello has been an activist all her life. Her
work has taken her to countries all around the world. She is a
current US global ambassador for the women of Haiti, and has
served on the Haiti Economic Development Advisory Panel. In
2009 Bello was voted one of *Variety* magazine's most powerful
women in Hollywood for her activism in Darfur. Growing up
just outside Philadelphia, she says her family situation showed
her the need for women to raise their voices.

By the age of twenty-four, my mother had four kids. She had a
nursing degree, thank goodness, but she expected never to work.
She wanted to be home and raise her kids. My father was a
construction worker and, unfortunately, when he was thirty he
broke his back and could never work again. My mother went
back to nursing to support our family.

So I grew up in a household with a female role model who was
working, and that's what I assumed women did. Because of that,
I noticed the psychological impact of a woman making more
money than a man, taking care of a man and especially this
big Italian man who could once lift a whole building and now
couldn't. And I saw the sexual politics playing out in my own

house. I didn't understand when I was younger the idea of a man feeling emasculated because a woman has the economic power, and it really created chaos in my family. My father just descended into a place of drug addiction and alcohol abuse, and wasn't able to contain his anger so took it out on his family. I think my feeling of justice, my fight for women's rights was born of that, the nest I came into.

As I got older I have always been an activist. I went to Villanova University to study peace and justice education, and worked at the Women's Law Project in Philadelphia studying women's rights.

Many years ago, when I was much younger, there was a hurricane in Nicaragua and I wanted to go and help. I didn't know how and I called Save the Children and got a group of friends, toys, glitter and arts. We ended up going to these villages where the people had had everything taken away from them and doing what artists do. We brought joy and played with the kids. The kids felt joy, so their communities felt 'Yes, we survived and, yes, there's a way through and, yes, there's still joy.' It gave them hope.

So I continued those travels and was in Kosovo during the war, going to the camps and talking to the women and the kids. Sitting in this huge warehouse dorm room with these beautiful women and hearing their stories about what they'd been through. Many of their husbands, boyfriends, brothers had been killed, while many of them had been raped. Some of the children walking around were children of rape. I brought nail polish, I brought a bag of make-up, and for hours we sat around doing each other's nails and make-up and hair and laughing. It might seem like such a simple thing, but it's a release in a lot of ways for women.

I do believe there's evil in this world, a lot of evil. I'm working with the Yazidi women who experienced the genocide in Iraq and Kurdistan. The women are taken as sex slaves by ISIS and are experiencing the most horrific thing. This one group of women stood up and said, 'They rape us, we kill them,' and they started their own militia. I'm doing a piece on them with some ladies, because they are going after ISIS to get their sisters back, to get vengeance. It's pure evil what these men are doing to women.

Maria Bello's activism continues in the US. The day after Donald Trump was sworn in as the 45th President of the United States, up to two million people took part in the Women's March in cities around the world. The protesters advocated progress on a host of issues, including human rights, racial equality, environmental improvements and the advancement of women's rights. Much of it was seen as a reaction to statements and policy pronouncements Trump had made on the campaign trail, threatening to roll back hard-won gains, and views regarded by many as offensive or anti-women. One such statement was dubbed 'Pussygate' after a tape emerged of Trump boasting that when you are a star women let you do anything, including forcefully grabbing them by the genitals. Maria Bello helped lead the march in Park City, Utah, and gave a headline-capturing speech, saying, 'When they try to punch you by grabbing your pussy, punch them back harder with your pussy power.' She sees the Women's March as the start of a new kind of activism across America.

I think a real complacency set in before the election, the assumption that things had been getting progressively better for women, in terms of equality, ownership of our bodies, pay equity – so I think a lot of people stayed home.

And after this man won, whom I will never call the president, I think that people have become activated. The Women's March was a huge, huge activator. To have so many people on the street, not only women but men, husbands, lovers. People who are standing up for justice, really. Justice and a way forward that is loving but powerful. We are not only fighting against something, we're fighting for something: we're fighting for the dignity and respect of all human beings.

I work with many different women's organisations. Since the Women's March, everyone's been asking, 'What can we do?' or 'What's the next step?' and 'Let's structure this. Let's make sure that this isn't just a hashtag on social media and you've done your bit.'

The Women's March organisers were so inspiring. They put together ten actions for the first hundred days, various calls and huddles that you could do in your community. We need to

collectively find a way to make it a definitive date. Here's the
date that women all over the world are showing up, this once-a-
month day to bring your community together, whether you're a
Democrat or a Republican or non-partisan. We all know women
love to gather and have fun, so how do we make that fun as
well as changing the economics of the situation, so that we are
supporting candidates who are doing particular work we
believe in? Supporting companies who support legislation we
believe in? Learning about them on that day and using your
money on that particular day to buy things that support what
you believe in.

Ruth Ibegbuna has worked with young people from some of
the most deprived areas of Manchester, teaching them leadership skills and helping them find their voice through the
RECLAIM project. Within RECLAIM, a group of girls who had
been victims of sexual abuse came together to challenge the
silence around child sexual exploitation.

It is a subject that has real resonance in the area after a
huge scandal was exposed in nearby Rochdale where nearly
fifty girls, some as young as thirteen, fell victim to a child
sexual abuse ring. The grooming gang targeted girls with chaotic
home lives, plied them with drink and drugs and repeatedly
raped and sexually assaulted them. A sexual-health worker
made more than 180 attempts over four years to get the police,
the council and social workers to take the abuse seriously.
However, the victims, from deprived and dysfunctional backgrounds, were dismissed as unreliable. Eventually nine men

were convicted of multiple offences. The Rochdale Safeguarding
Children Board highlighted failures by seventeen agencies that
were meant to protect the children, and the police apologised
for their inaction.

Ibegbuna believes that women have to take activism into
uncomfortable spaces if we're going to stop sexual abuse in
future.

*I've worked with girls who've been victims of child sexual
exploitation (CSE) and victims of the Rochdale grooming
scandal. Something that appalled me to my core at every level.
I feel that as women we can do better to support girls, full stop,
but especially vulnerable girls who need our help the most. I
would like to see UK movements of women supporting vulnerable girls far more effectively. That hasn't happened and it's
profoundly disappointing.*

*I think people turn away from CSE because it's uncomfortable.
The victims are often difficult for us to cope with. I think it
highlights mass failings that no one wants to own up to. It's
going to provoke some difficult conversations about communities, race and culture, and sometimes in Britain we shy away
from conversations that feel too difficult. And therefore we're
leaving twelve-, thirteen- and fourteen-year-old girls to fend for
themselves in terrible circumstances.*

*We don't want to hear about it. It's an uncomfortable truth.
But when you look at the number of child abuse victims, the*

number of women who have been sexually assaulted in this country, those numbers are staggering. We can no longer pretend that this is something that happens to other people, because it's happening to everyone. I think the more we talk about this, the more that we allow our young girls to believe that it's okay to discuss what is happening to them – to disclose it knowing they will be supported – that's the start of dealing with it. Stop pretending that things happen in isolation. They don't. Everything is interconnected.

There's a sense that until it was unavoidable, when society had to start facing up to CSE and dealing with it, we turned a blind eye. A lot of people turned a blind eye, institutions turned a blind eye, and even now, it's still going on.

I think that the power of women in this country could be utilised very powerfully to protect our vulnerable girls. I'm not sure that we've cracked that, and that, I think, is a shame.

Activism means different things to different people, whether it is starting a petition on a local issue or joining thousands on the internet to say #timesup. Championing a cause can sometimes be lonely, especially if it has received little media attention or has already been defeated in a parliament. However, by reclaiming new media, it is easier than ever for women to find other women who are already working in the same field somewhere in the world and to swap support, advice and best-practice ideas. As the cultural anthropologist Margaret Mead said: 'Never doubt that a small group of thoughtful, committed citizens can change the world; indeed, it's the only thing that ever has.'

KERRY KENNEDY
President,

Robert F Kennedy Human Rights

Kerry Kennedy is the daughter of assassinated US senator and former attorney general, Robert F. Kennedy, and presides over the human rights organisation set up in his name. As a writer and activist, she has pressed governments around the world on issues as diverse as freedom of expression, women's rights and judicial independence. She serves on the board of the US Institute of Peace and is chair of the Amnesty International USA Leadership Council. Among the many awards she has received for her work, she has been named Woman of the Year by Save the Children, Humanitarian of the Year by the South Asian Media Awards Foundation and has received the Eleanor Roosevelt Medal of Honor.

66 I had an appreciation of human rights at a very young age. My father was the seventh of nine. I was the seventh of eleven. In that situation, you think about fairness and about what's happening when somebody doesn't have too much power!

When I was a very young child, it was the height of the civil rights movement. My parents didn't separate their home from their work life – and so our household was always filled with civil-rights activists, with farm-worker activists from the Latino community, with Native Americans, student leaders and revolutionaries from around the world. There were always people in our living room, at our dining-table and playing football with us who were trying to create change.

One of my father's aides said you could sum up Dad's life with 'Get your boot off his neck.' And I think he spent a lot of his time doing that. It had an influence on me. When I was very young – three or four years old – when I was learning to tie my shoes, I made sure that if I put on the left one first, I tied the right one first because that was fair. I didn't want to favour one side over the other. Where does a child that age get that notion, if not from their parents? That concept of fairness.

When I was in college, I took an internship at Amnesty International. I documented abuses committed by US immigration officials, and I was horrified to find my country was treating the most destitute with such disdain. I wanted to do something about it.

I thought it was unfair. Then I read the Universal Declaration of Human Rights and that document changed my life. I realised that all of the chaotic things that had happened in my life – the political assassinations of my uncle and my father, the attacks on women, like the rape of two of my best friends in high school, the attacks on the LGBT community, the death of a close friend who was gay, not out of the closet because it was too dangerous, and one of the first to die from HIV/AIDS – had one thing in common: they were violations of human rights and I could use that document to create change. I decided to go to law school and spend my life doing that. And I've been doing it for the last thirty-five years.

The role of men and women is interesting in my family. When I was growing up, my mother was clear about the role of women. Women stay at home and raise children. The boys take out the garbage, the girls do the dishes. No kidding. She was horrified by the women's rights movement. She was a big sports fan and believed that women could never compete like men do. Meanwhile, she was running a household with eleven kids. She was also running a non-profit organisation with people from across the country working for her. She was on the board of several different organisations that she basically ran. She was the only woman on the NFL Charity Committee, which she also ran. So she was saying one thing and doing another.

Then we had other role models, like my aunt who started the Special Olympics, my aunt who was the ambassador to Northern Ireland and my grandmother, Rose Kennedy, who was so mighty, so powerful and such a strong influence on our family and in our lives. So there was rhetoric and there was reality. And I think we all learned from reality. **"**

RUTH IBEGBUNA
Founder and CEO, RECLAIM

Ruth Ibegbuna's single focus is to enable young people from deprived backgrounds to achieve their full potential. Since it was formed in 2007, RECLAIM, her Manchester-based charity, has helped equip nearly a thousand young people with the skills, confidence and all-round fearlessness they need to achieve their dreams. Focusing on 'disruptive leadership', she encourages her young charges to feel as at home in Parliament or the boardroom as they do in their communities.

❝ I worked for a year at a very exclusive boarding school in Manchester, then moved to work in Moss Side, which was two and a half miles down the road. In both schools I worked with some fantastic young people who were as bright as each other, and I was morally outraged at the difference in outcomes for children from within three miles of each other. So, the philosophy behind RECLAIM has always been about finding young people who have leadership potential – with possibly the wrong postcodes, because they're from working-class backgrounds – and giving them the opportunities to shine and to have the confidence to go out there and be leaders.

Young people from working-class communities are quite often super-confident within their communities, with big voices in their schools, big voices in their families. But when they're taken out of those familiar surroundings into a space that feels posh or alien or full of people who don't share their values, quite often that confidence diminishes and they lose out to young people who, from the age of five, have been taught how to display leadership ability.

Often when our young people are taken out of their communities, they shrink back. They feel, This is not my place. I've not got the right to be here. They go to the Houses of Parliament and think, This is for kids from Eton. They don't believe they have the right to be heard in any space. We are constantly trying to disrupt that narrative with them and take them to lots of different places. It's about having the confidence to know that your authentic voice is valid and people will want to listen to what you've got to say.

The girls are growing up much quicker than the boys. And emotionally they're much more mature. When we first started, we asked the children, 'How do you see your life evolving? What do you want to do?' Twelve-year-old boys all want to play football, they all want to play for United – which is fine. When you start talking to the girls about their aspirations, they undersell themselves. The boys all see themselves as the next Messi, but what I find heartbreaking about the girls is that their ambitions aren't big enough for their talent. So a girl will say she wants to be a hairdresser. Fine, cool – but we know that she could go on to own a range of salons if she wanted to. Or the girls just want to ensure that their family are happy and healthy, which is wonderful but there's very little putting themselves into it. So a lot of the work we do with girls has to be about finding their own voice and path, and realising that they're not just a vehicle for someone else's happiness.

Quite often when families are struggling, girls tend to be confidantes of Mum, while boys are sent out of the house to play with their mates. We've found that many of our girls are absorbing a lot of the stresses within their families, while the boys are acting out those stresses outside. The girls seem to be far more aware of tensions in their domestic sphere and are far more restrained in their ambitions. It worries me that some won't go on to fulfil their potential, because they will never explore what that potential actually is or means.

I think it's interesting, but also quite sad. **"**

Women of the World

Women face challenges the world over. But those challenges vary hugely in nature and scale from country to country. There is tremendous work going on by women for women to make things better. In this chapter I showcase three of the many organisations that are making the biggest difference in some of the world's toughest places.

We know the world is not equal for men and women. We've known it for a long time. It's not just physiologically that we see the difference between the sexes, but in almost every measure – educational opportunities, political representation, employability, earning potential, health outcomes, likelihood of suffering sexual violence, cultural capital and community status. And while in the developed world the visible campaigns we see are for more women in boardrooms or to cut the gender pay gap, in many of the world's developing nations, the differences are far more stark and the outcomes shocking.

According to the United Nations, every minute a young woman somewhere in the world is infected with HIV. Early pregnancy and childbirth are a leading cause of death for girls aged from fifteen to nineteen in developing countries. Right now, 140 million women, who want to stop or delay child-bearing, have no access to family planning. Child marriage, genital mutilation and violence against women are still cultural practices in a number of countries. Other developing nations restrict women's economic empowerment, denying them the right to own land, inherit property or have access to a bank account and credit.

Oxfam has studied the economic differences between men and women around the globe. Unsurprisingly, they conclude that the majority of the world's poor are women. The reasons for this are many, but the ability to work and the rate of pay in employment play a major role. Globally, 700 million fewer women are in paid work than men. For the many, many millions who are in sustained employment, women are more likely to be in the lowest-paid jobs. The difference in income between the sexes is around 24 per cent, and the gap is narrowing so slowly that Oxfam estimates that 170 years will have passed before women's pay catches up with men's.

The issue doesn't stop with paid employment. The amount of unpaid care work – looking after children, the elderly or sick – done by women is many multiples of that performed by men. The global value of this work each year is estimated at $10 trillion – which is equivalent to one-eighth of the world's entire GDP. Because this unpaid work often takes place on top of paid employment, women's working days are far longer.

That means, when added together, a young woman starting out now will work the equivalent of four more years than a man over her lifetime.

I cannot conceive what it would be like to be denied schooling. Or to be sold in marriage at fourteen. I cannot imagine being unable to take decisions about my own life, or even my own body. The thought of my unborn child becoming ill sometime in the future frightens me already – never mind the worry that I might not be able to provide him or her with enough food, safe drinking water or access to medicine. Yet these are the situations facing hundreds of millions of women across the world today.

I know how vulnerable I felt even in that small BBC pay dispute – and the BBC is an employer that had its own codified values and standards. Even though it took place in a leading Western nation, with the rule of law, equal-pay legislation and an employment-tribunal system, I still felt exposed and had to force myself to ask for more money. How can women in countries with no legal protection, no status in the workplace and no access to representation possibly address the systemic economic unfairness they face every day? How can women who are seen culturally as the property of their husbands assert their sexual and reproductive rights within a marriage? How can a daughter argue that she deserves the same amount of schooling as her brothers when none of her female relatives was permitted the same?

Nearly two decades ago, the world pledged to step in: 191 individual countries and 22 international organisations signed up to the United Nations' Millennium Development Goals. In eight distinct areas, covering poverty, education, health, equality and the environment, measurable improvements were promised by 2015. Now the numbers are in, we can see how far we've come.

The biggest success has been in tackling global poverty. The aim was to halve the number of people living in extreme poverty – on less than $1.25 per day – by 2015. The target was hit five years ahead of schedule. This change is the biggest leap forward in poverty reduction in recent history and has had a huge effect on women, who are disproportionately likely to be impoverished.

Good progress has been made in girls' primary education, too. While ensuring universal participation was always going to be a big task, enrolment rates at primary schools passed 90 per cent in 2011 and have kept growing, if slowly. However, the dropout rates mean a sizeable number of children aren't completing primary school. UN research across sixty-three developing countries shows girls were more likely to be out of school than boys among primary and lower secondary age groups. The gender gap in school attendance widens with age, irrespective of household income. By college or university, only 4 per cent of developing countries see broad parity between male and female entrants.

One goal that has been missed for women is the halting of the spread of HIV/AIDS and making sure that everyone infected has access to treatment. While there has been a steady decline in the incidence of HIV in most areas, the number of women living with the virus has been climbing for over a decade. Globally, women aged fifteen to twenty-four have a 50 per cent higher risk of becoming infected with HIV compared to their male peers. The UN says the low economic and social status of women in many countries means they are often at a disadvantage when it comes to negotiating safer sex and accessing HIV prevention services.

Similarly, there has been disappointment when it comes to child and maternal mortality. The aim was to reduce the number of children dying before the age of five by two-thirds and to cut by three-quarters the number of women who die in pregnancy and from birth-related issues. Both have seen a reduction, but by nowhere near enough to get close to the goal.

The World Health Organization says that more than 800 women die every day from preventable causes related to pregnancy and childbirth, with 99 per cent of all maternal deaths occurring in developing countries. Maternal mortality is higher in women living in rural areas and among poorer communities, while young teenagers are most at risk. One in three maternal deaths related to pregnancy and childbirth could be avoided if women who wanted effective contraception had access to it. Around the world, women are dying because they are unable to make decisions about their own body.

It's something the Bill and Melinda Gates Foundation sees every day. Although she was raised as a Catholic in a religious part of Texas and educated by nuns, Melinda Gates's work around the world has led her to recognise birth control as a key component of the holy trinity of female empowerment: health, education and economic independence.

❝ *You have to start with health. If women and their kids don't have basic good health, you lock them into a cycle of poverty. If*

you don't have good health, you can't go learn and then partici-
pate in society.

So they need to have good health. Then they need to take
decisions, and to be able to do that you need to have some
empowerment in your life. If you're educated you're better able
to decide how you educate your kids, how you'll interact with
the health system. Then they need economic empowerment. And
if you get those three things going – health, decision-making/
education and economic empowerment – it literally unlocks the
cycle of poverty for these women. But you need to help them
get on that path so they can lift themselves up.

If you look at countries that have made the progression from
low income to middle income, you will see the importance of
investing in family planning. If a woman doesn't know enough
about her body and has no access to family planning, she will
have more kids than she often wants and is locked into the
cycle of poverty. If she has four, five, six kids and can't feed
them, she cannot educate them or go on to get a job. We know
in the United States and the UK that if a woman has access to
contraceptives she can space her children as she wants, which
gives her the chance to live the life she wants – to participate
in the workforce, to go to college. It starts there with that tool.
If she doesn't have access to that tool she won't to be able to
live the full life she wants to live.

The longitudinal study into global health that took place in
the 1970s in Bangladesh was one of the best that has been
done. It gave a series of villages access to voluntary family
planning, taught women about it, and compared the result with
seven villages that were not included. In the villages that had

access to contraceptives, the women were healthier, the children were healthier and the families were wealthier. It changed the cycle of poverty. They had a chance to lift themselves out of it.

If a woman is educated, the entire way in which she will access the system for her children and herself completely changes. Because she's literate, she can ask different questions. The ways in which she views authority change. The way in which she will ask a question of someone in authority changes and she may be better able to carry out what they tell her, if it's pills she or her kids need to take or instructions she should follow about coming for antenatal checks. The education that started at primary level helps with health. It also helps give her a voice, her decision-making authority in her own family and community. Education is a key lever for everything else we care about in health and economic empowerment. And those three wheels, health, decision-making/education and economic empowerment, need to spin together to ultimately help a woman lift her family out of poverty.

Increasing financial empowerment is a huge task. But Gates believes it is crucial in ensuring genuine societal change, which increases the standing of women in the community, reduces domestic violence and offers the next generation of girls a transformed future.

In some countries, a woman wasn't welcomed at the bank. She couldn't get on the bus. With digital financial services and a device she can take money on, now she can save a dollar or two each day. Before, no one would welcome her at the bank with two dollars a day, even if she could get there. Now when the school fees are due, she knows she's contributing.

There are already certain studies to show that when a woman has access to her own account, separate from her husband's, she invests differently in her children, but we're learning too that the way in which she participates in the economy is different. Her chance of getting a job changes if she sees herself as a saver and is saving money. That has profound implications for the next twenty years for women's empowerment. When she has access to her own resources, it changes how her mother-in-law views her, how her husband views her, how her son views her because she can buy him a bicycle to get to school. It changes a lot.

I talk to women in India, in villages, and they have said to me, 'Before no one knew my name. The only person who knew my name was me, but now everyone in this village knows my name. I feel empowered. I feel like my sisters, and I can go to the police and say, 'This rape case: we demand our rights. It has to be tried.' Or 'We're due a health clinic in our village. We just have to build one.' Her view of herself changes and the community's view changes around her.

Just as the Bill and Melinda Gates Foundation has entire programmes directed towards advancing the situation of women in numerous countries, so Robert F. Kennedy Human Rights operates globally. Among its many projects, it has helped overturn laws in Uganda making homosexuality punishable by life in prison without parole, and has partnered with local human rights lawyers to address the persecution of women in

South America. Its president, Kerry Kennedy, explains its approach to advancing women's rights by tackling gender violence:

The first thing RFK Human Rights does is hold governments accountable for human-rights abuses. We do that specifically with women throughout Central America, which has three of the five countries in the world (two of which are Sudan and Syria) where it's most dangerous to be a woman – three countries in Central America. One of those is Guatemala.

In the last thirty years about 2 per cent of the women murdered in Guatemala have had their cases brought to trial. Of those, only about 5 per cent ended with a conviction. So, basically, if you kill women there, nothing happens to you.

The killing of women because they are women is called femicide and RFK Human Rights brought the first successful case regarding femicide against the Guatemala government. And we won. We won in the Inter American Court – which is the Supreme Court that sits above the Supreme Courts of all the Latin American governments. In that case, the judgment said the government of Guatemala had to make certain changes. They had to buy a certain number of rape crisis kits. They had to put streetlights on streets. They had to do women's rights training with police officers. They had to do a whole series of things. We've just brought a similar suit in Mexico, which we are putting through the courts now.

So, we take cases like that. That's one part of what we do. The second thing we do relates to the hundred largest economies on earth. Fifty per cent of them are corporations. So, we work with investors and corporations on women's rights. As an example, we did a survey of the thirty largest university endowments in the United States. They include Harvard, Yale, Stanford, Duke – all the largest universities. And we asked them, 'What percentage of your endowment dollars is invested by women and minorities?'

And the answer was 1.1 per cent. And these are universities. These are entities where the goal of the organisation is integration, non-discrimination. We're now working with those universities to correct that issue.

This is very, very important. It's not a big surprise to anybody in the investment business – there's about $77 trillion in the investment business worldwide and about 2 per cent worldwide is controlled by women. Women are being excluded and therefore cannot make the decisions about which types of companies get investment, and the investment industry is where capital is accumulated in our world today.

So you're getting all these charitable dollars decided upon by old white men, instead of women and members of minority communities, who are most impacted by social injustice and, therefore, should be in most control of how money is spent on these issues.

Number three. If we get the governments and corporations to behave themselves, it's for nought if we don't bring along the next generation. So we have a human rights education programme which we teach to 1.2 million students worldwide each year. And we're really teaching students about their rights and how to assert them. To have them create change in society. That's our work.

One of the greatest disruptors of advancement is war. The suspension of the normal rules of society leaves women particularly vulnerable. Dr Rola Hallam's work in setting up hospitals in war-torn Syria has allowed her to see how the role of women has changed in her home country. The march of women's rights isn't always in a state of advance – especially with organisations like ISIS attempting to create an Islamic state in the country. But Dr Hallam says the hardship hasn't stopped women fighting for their place in Syria, despite the conflict and rape being used as a weapon of war.

In communities where religion, honour and such things are of profound importance, rape is a very clever tool to use to drive people out. People would leave not just because of the bombing or the violence, but 'If my daughters or my wife are at risk of getting raped, well, I'm better off going on the move and avoiding that.' So it's a very efficient tool.

Right at the beginning in Syria, a lot of women were involved in the non-violent movement and the protests. The revolution really woke up the masses, and in the early days of the protest you would see men alongside women. Women were definitely playing an important role in that. Thereafter, as the violence spread, a lot of the women carried on as part of the non-violence movement, and some joined the defensive movement. The Syrian regime had a women's unit, and female fighters were part of the original defensive FSA [Free Syrian Army] Force.

But I would say that the majority of women were trying to create Syrian civil society. Before the revolution and the war, there was no Syrian civil society. Syria was under a dictator-

ship: the only civil society or NGOs had to be sanctioned by the regime, under the patronship of Mrs Assad or someone like that.

Despite the restrictions of operating under a state of extreme conflict, the work of charities, media organisations and NGOs during the war has seen the level of state control shift and has changed the role of women.

We have played a humungous part in the creation and growth of Syrian civil society. Within that, there's the aid sector, citizen journalists, and the women's rights-, peace- and security-related sectors.

We've seen the role of women in Syria change dramatically as many of them have become widows and heads of households. Suddenly women who'd had no education or jobs are now female heads of households having to look after enormous numbers of children and elderly parents but without the means to do that. They were already the pillars of the family, but now they have become central in so many ways. But, sadly, with Islamicisation, we've also seen – through the regime and through ISIS – this quest to crush, objectify and oppress them.

For women in the Middle East, we are fighting patriarchy, and that these women are seen only through the single story of their oppression: women have to wear a burka, they have no rights, they're looked at as secondary human beings almost. And I find that really frustrating because not only is it a single story, it's a minority story. In the Middle East, and in Syria specifically, we're fighting the patriarchy, we're fighting these prejudices, but we're trying to do it while dodging bullets and bombs.

The way in which organisations are effecting change is, in itself, changing. Very few of the big NGOs still work to a model where disaster aid or development work is carried out by people from (usually Western) donor countries who fly to an affected country, operate in a silo and fly out once the project is finished. From enormous philanthropic organisations, like the Bill and Melinda Gates Foundation, to small charities such as Dr Hallam's Hand in Hand for Syria, development agencies now make a point of partnering with local people or organisations. Partly to encourage community buy-in, but also to build skills and resilience, this model should increase the impact of aid, and ensure its benefits continue, even after projects have finished. There are some truly inspiring women working to make the lives of many other women better.

Consultant anaesthetist Rola Hallam saves lives. Since the conflict in Syria began, she has been at the forefront of efforts to protect the civilian population from the forces of President Bashar al-Assad. Through the charity Hand in Hand for Syria, she has helped build hospitals in areas bombed by the regime. Her own organisation, CanDo, helps local health workers and humanitarians provide treatment and services in war-devastated communities. She lectures at the London School of Economics and is an international human rights advocate.

"We moved to the UK from Syria when I was thirteen, not speaking any English. I'd always known I was going to be a doctor from when I was very little and it seemed for a while that my lack of English would stop me doing that. When it came to applying for university, all my teachers advised me I should apply for chemistry or biology because my grades weren't good enough. They said you need straight As to apply to medical school and I had to remind them sternly but politely that I'd only learned English two years ago and they should give me a break and let me have a chance at applying. I thought that was absolutely ridiculous.

One university offered me an interview and I got the place. It was the medical school at the Royal Free Hospital, where I am now a consultant. That was a very early lesson: it showed me that how we perceive our potential is what our potential will be. If you want something, you work damn hard towards it, then fight tooth and nail for it.

So off I went on my medical career. From a very early stage I'd known that global health was going to be an important facet of my work. I think when you grow up in a resource-poor setting and you have a deeply ingrained sense of justice, you can either push the medical frontier or you can be at the back making sure no one's left behind. I felt that that was my role.

I worked in sub-Saharan Africa, mainly training health-care workers in anaesthesia and how better to manage critically ill children. And I really thought that was where my life was heading, until the revolution started in Syria, then the war, and my life turned upside down.

At the beginning, helping with the aid effort was very low level – we had bandages and blood bags, anti-tetanus shots and antibiotics, and tried to distribute them to the communities that we knew were affected. Then, as the violence and the war spread, it soon became apparent that individuals' small efforts were insufficient and we really needed to organise and join forces to better our response as Syrians.

Around 2012 I joined a newly formed Syrian-led British organisation called Hand in Hand for Syria as a volunteer but took on the role of medical director, creating our medical humanitarian response.

We would be told by one community, 'We're now close to one of the front lines and we don't have a trauma centre or a triage centre or a first-aid post.' In another area we were told they needed a children's hospital as there were no children's health facilities. My role was to go to those areas and do the needs assessment, collecting the data, speaking to the communities, and mapping the health-care facilities that were or were not available. With Hand in Hand for Syria, and another couple of Syrian organisations, I have helped to set up six hospitals in the north of the country.

It used to be very easy for me to go in and out. Then it became harder. Then, with the Islamicisation and the spread of rape as a weapon of war, I needed to wear a hijab and alter my dress so that I looked less Western and more like the locals. War, especially for people like me, raises the question of identity. I was going to Syria and was looked upon there as an outsider. Suddenly I wasn't British enough for the British and I wasn't Syrian enough for the Syrians. I experienced a moment of crisis: 'What the hell am I? I don't appear to be included in either domain.' **"**

How Far We've Come.
How Far We've
Got to Go

My birthday is on 10 November. It's an entirely unremarkable date, except that, according to the Fawcett Society, it is also the current Equal Pay Day for the United Kingdom: the day when women stop earning relative to men because of the gender pay gap. And, in the UK, it's been on 10 November for the last three years. The 14.1 per cent gender pay gap for women in full-time work has not narrowed one iota in that time. We might have seen our first female lord chancellor appointed in those three years, the first female Church of England bishop and the second female prime minister, but for the ordinary working woman, there has been not a single pound or penny of advance. Nothing.

This year also marked the centenary of women getting the

vote in the UK. Or, at least, some women. When it comes to the celebrations, statue unveilings, TV programmes, exhibitions and displays that have gone on around the country, we should be clear about what the 1918 Representation of the People Act actually meant.

A hundred years ago, the UK Parliament decided a select group of women – and most men – were finally to be included in the franchise for UK general elections: women over the age of thirty who were householders, the wives of householders, occupiers of property with an annual rent of five pounds, or graduates voting in university constituencies were considered responsible enough to vote. This amounted to around about 8.4 million women.

My great-grandmother, Bessie Ritchie, wouldn't have been among them. Despite hurdling the age barrier, despite raising five sons to adulthood (she also had a daughter, who died young), she didn't qualify – leaving school at fourteen and living in a Glasgow Corporation tenement in Tradeston, she had neither the means nor the education to be deemed worthy of political decision-making.

Voting wasn't a universal right but a value judgement, given only to those thought up to the task. It would take another ten years before universal suffrage was achieved – equal voting rights between men and women, offered to all over twenty-one, irrespective of property. So, for me, this year's centenary should be less of a celebration in itself, and more about marking a staging post to a better system. And some huge advances have been made in the last hundred years.

In 1918, women were still barred from practising law; now,

more than 50 per cent of the country's lawyers are female. The first paid female police officers in the Metropolitan Police didn't come into service until February 1919, a year after the first women got the vote. Now the Met is headed by its first ever female commissioner.

It took until 1921 for the University of Oxford – and 1947 for Cambridge – to admit women to degrees. Last year, for the first time ever, female Cambridge applicants received more offers of places than males. And in Parliament, where the Representation of the People Act inspired gender reforms across so many sectors of the UK, the first woman was elected to the House of Commons in 1918; in last year's snap general election, a record 208 women MPs were returned.

All of this demonstrates progress, but it doesn't point to parity. Even if we take those 208 MPs and add them to every single woman elected to the Commons in history, we still wouldn't be able to fill the famous green benches. In a hundred years, the United Kingdom has returned just 489 female MPs in a parliament of 650, elected every four or five years.

However, the seeds are there for ever greater progress. Looking at the university admission numbers for subjects such as law and medicine, where women dwarf men, it's easy to envisage the boys' network crumbling within the professions. Looking at schools, the GCSE pass rate for girls is nearly ten points higher than it is for boys, which signposts a potential future where more women qualify for more jobs and the gender employment gap is scythed away.

The indicators for long-term progress are positive in many areas. But the idea of 'equal' exists only if women are given the same platform to progress, the same reward for hard work and the same treatment in the job as the men standing next to them.

And this is just the view from the UK.

According to the UN, the inequalities faced by women can start at birth and follow them their whole lives. Sometimes to deadly effect. In countries where girls are deprived of access to proper nutrition or healthcare, we see higher rates of female mortality. Similarly, girls are disproportionately affected by issues such as child marriage or genital mutilation. Across the world, nearly 15 million girls under the age of eighteen are married every year. That's 37,000 child brides every day. It's estimated that 133 million girls and women – mostly in Africa and the Middle East – have been subjected to some form of female genital mutilation or cutting. Female genital mutilation carries a much higher risk of infertility, birthing problems, prolonged bleeding, infection (including HIV) and death.

Women's life chances can also be limited by violence. United Nations research states that more than a third of women have been subjected to physical or sexual violence either by a partner or by an outside assailant. That is at least a billion people who have been attacked.

Politically, women are far behind when it comes to their voices being heard, or decisions being taken. As of October 2013, women made up just over 20 per cent of parliamentarians in single or lower houses of parliament, and just under 20 per cent in senates or upper houses. While this marks an improvement over the last fifteen years, the pace of change is so slow it will take nearly four decades to reach the parity zone.

The one thing that will help close the gender gap for future generations is getting education correct. That simply isn't happening. In the developing world, only about a third of countries offer equality to children of primary school age. At secondary school, the gap is even wider.

The UN tracks 130 countries around the world to check how well progress is being achieved. Currently, only two have achieved gender parity at all levels of education. And this difference matters and will affect people for their whole lives. With fewer girls going to school, and those who do attend staying in education for a shorter period than boys, the gender skills gap leads to fewer job opportunities. This results in women having a far reduced earning power than men. Men earn, on average, 24 per cent more than women, a disparity that remains stubbornly wide.

Theresa May is only the second female prime minister in UK political history and one of only two female leaders in the G20 group of leading economic nations. When talking of Britain's social progress over the last hundred years, she has referred to her own background. Both her grandmothers were domestic servants, and it is a matter of pride to the family that there are three professors and a prime minister among those women's grandchildren.

❝ *During the women's suffrage centenary events, I met Helen Pankhurst, the great-granddaughter of Emmeline, and visited the Pankhurst home in Manchester. My godmother's mother, Ernestine Mills, was a suffragette with the Pankhursts, and her father had been a doctor to members of the Pankhurst family. Those women who campaigned for the vote, I don't know whether they envisaged a female prime minister at some stage, or if it was just the first injustice they wanted to deal with. But I think we have come on enormously.*

It's great that we've got a second female prime minister, and that there are more women in Parliament, but in politics and elsewhere there's still a job to be done in overcoming the innate sense of 'This is what we expect a man to do' and 'This is what we expect a woman to do'. In business, there's a real challenge to get more women through the corporate pipeline and onto boards, rather than just as non-executive directors. It's related to the experience women have. Often the men have come via the finance and operational route, women through government affairs or human resources. Skill sets may be slightly different. People may approach jobs in different ways: it doesn't mean it's any less valid or that you don't get results.

There are areas we've got to watch – like the gender pay gap. We've acted in relation to companies reporting on it, but we've got to make sure the dial actually moves.

I'm pleased that we've introduced flexible parental leave and the right to request flexible working. I think it's important what we've done in the areas of injustice which affect women propor-tionately more – the new Domestic Violence Act we're bringing in, addressing modern slavery – and areas like female genital mutilation as well. It's always a question of 'What are you actu-ally doing for people?'

For many, the pace of chance is not nearly fast enough. Three years ago Sandi Toksvig co-founded the Women's Equality Party because, in her view, none of the UK's main political parties were serious about prioritising women's equality:

I'm an angry feminist. I had been gathering women's history and researching women's history all of my life because I felt there were not enough role models. Every time I spoke to a politician about the situation for women in this country it was always 'Yes, yes, something needs to be done, but not now.' There was always something more important, more worthwhile. It has always, always, always been put on the back burner.

And I'd had enough. Every year I host a celebration of International Women's Day called Mirth Control where I gather the world's only all-female orchestra, who play music composed entirely by women, and I give a lecture about some aspect of women's history.

Three years ago I decided to gather a cabinet of great women I thought we'd have in the cabinet if we could choose. Tanni Grey-Thompson was my sports minister, Helena Kennedy, the eminent lawyer, was lord chancellor – it was just a fabulous collection of astonishing women. At the same time, but unbeknown to me, the journalist and author Catherine Mayer was at a meeting that was looking at where women are politically – the lack of representation of women in Parliament, on boards, in leadership positions and so on – and Catherine said, 'Maybe we need to start our own political party,' because a pressure group wasn't enough.

She phoned me and said, 'Sandi, I want you to join me and start this political party.'

I said, 'But I'm already doing it on stage with my cabinet. Why don't we make it an actual thing?'

I left the BBC's News Quiz programme to start the party.

The fact that it was needed came home to me at the last mayoral elections in London. There were seven candidates, and Sophie Walker, the eighth, was the Women's Equality candidate. The first seven did not know that Sophie would speak at the hustings and all gave their five-minute talk to the audience. Not one – including Sadiq Khan – mentioned anything to do with the women of London. Not a word. Not a single word about childcare, about the issue of equal pay, anything to do with women.

And then Sophie stood up. 'You understand that this is one of the worst cities in the world to be a woman? You get that, right?' But nobody had mentioned it, and then I knew, yeah, it's no good being a pressure group, we need to be an actual political party.

And, wow, we're on a fantastic trajectory. We're the only party in the world that hopes one day not to exist. One day, we hope we'll be done. I say to every party, 'Steal our policies. Please, help yourself.'

We have costed everything. We have costed childcare. We have costed how to close the gender pay gap. We have worked out what we need to do. If you want to do it, please just crack on. The Women's Equality Party is not partisan. We're not left, we're not right. We're about solving the problem.

Toksvig finds marking the centenary of some women's enfranchisement a hollow celebration. She says the need to start a new party to advance the pursuit of equality is a damning indictment of the pace of change.

Actually, this is an anniversary that I didn't particularly want to celebrate. It made me depressed. There still isn't the representation we need. Two hundred women at the BBC having to say, 'Please can we have the same pay as the boys'? It's shocking.

I'm still very angry. Still full of fury. I'm sixty – you think I'd be calming down. I get angrier.

There's so much more to be done. I am a mix between relentlessly depressed by how much there is to be done, and heartened that our party has grown.

It's not huge. We have eight full-time members of staff, but we have offices and our volunteer force is phenomenal. We are reaching women who have not volunteered for a party before or not voted before. Have not felt engaged before.

The Labour Party sent a pink bus out, trying to get people to vote. Please, please, please – do not do that to women. Treat them as grown-ups.

Frances O'Grady is the general secretary of the British Trades Union Congress, which brings fifty of the UK's trade unions together, representing millions of workers. The TUC has fought to enhance workers' rights since it was founded more than 150 years ago and the movement has charted changes in employment law and practice over that time. As the first female TUC general secretary, O'Grady acknowledges that, as well as employers, trade unionism has had to change with the times. She believes every new age brings new challenges for women, and it's not always about the law: new technology can impact on employment practice too.

Job segregation is still really stark. It's often accompanied by who's got bargaining power. There are those who believe on all parts of the spectrum that women work for pin money, that they should put up and shut up, and their job is to stand by their men. And those who believe workers will be stronger if we are not divided, whether that's by gender or race or nationality or anything, but stick together and win equality with each other. Then it's harder for the exploitative boss to divide and rule.

But things have shifted in the sense that women's lives have changed. They have fewer babies, later. So, the motherhood penalty on pay kicks in later. On the other hand, women and men, but predominantly women, are also looking after elderly parents and the pay gap is actually at its widest when women reach their fifties because they are doing the double, as women always are.

Of course, this is also about what men do, and mothers at work are always going to feel more stressed unless they're with somebody who is also prepared to phone in to work and say, 'Sorry, the kids have got measles, I can't make it in today.' I see more of an appetite among men to play more of a role but I'm not sure that's changed sufficiently to make life easier for women

There are other kinds of changes. Heavy industry has gone, but gender segregation seems to kick in in new ways. So young women are more likely to be stuck on insecure contracts. It's not just what that means for pay packets or contracts of employment. We put out a big survey last year on sexual harassment that showed two-thirds of young women experience some form of sexual harassment, including everything from unwelcome jokes and comments right through to sexual assault.

But, of course, when women are on zero hours or agency contracts, their ability to push back is much more difficult. What was really upsetting for me was the number of young women who just left. So it's never reported, never challenged, and they end up losing their jobs. So it seems to me there are still those kinds of industrial and occupational divisions, but I also think the big division in Britain today is between insecure and secure employment and women are more likely to get stuck in insecure work and that's a problem, a big problem.

The first thing to say is that flexibility is great. Lots of people, particularly women, often really value flexibility. The problem is when it's all on the boss's terms and it isn't two-way. Now technology means we're seeing 'just in time' labour in the way that we've seen 'just in time' production. It's not only about the Ubers of this world and the gig economy. Simply being on the end of a mobile phone and waiting to be called into work is now possible in a way it wouldn't have been in the past because low-paid workers all have smartphones. They have to, that's how they get their work, but they're hanging around waiting to see whether they're going to get called in.

Just like those workers who had to hang around at the factory gate or on the quayside, they are not getting paid for that time – only in some ways it's worse because at least they were day labourers. Zero-hours workers aren't guaranteed any hours, not even an hour or two, never mind a day.

We've got care workers travelling between appointments who are not even getting the national minimum wage, or workers at

*warehouses being searched in their own time – body searches,
as well. Think what that means for young women in terms of
their experience of work. So the potential for a much more
oppressive regime is there with new technology in a way that
maybe it wasn't quite there previously.*

*All our work shows that the problem has grown. We've got a
much bigger proportion of the workforce in what we would
define as extreme exploitation, not just low paid but also insecure
hours and no rights or very few rights – whether that's sham
self-employment or zero hours – where you don't even have the
right to a payslip or a contract of employment, let alone anything
else. Even if you had rights, would you feel able to enforce them,
or are you going to be afraid that if you stick your head above
the parapet you won't get offered another day's work?*

O'Grady has dedicated her working life to improve the working
lives of others. Her campaigns to educate, empower and improve
conditions for women have made a huge difference to the
opportunities and wage packets of thousands of British workers.
But the struggle to make things better for current and future
generations does not stop at the water's edge of the UK. Nor
is it confined to treatment within the workplace. Kerry Kennedy
has spent decades lobbying governments and corporations as
the head of Robert F. Kennedy Human Rights. She has seen
wholesale change in the way in which women's rights are
recognised and discussed across the globe:

*When I started working on human rights – which was 1980 –
women's rights were not on the international agenda. It wasn't*

really until 1995 when Hillary Clinton went to Beijing and announced, 'Women's rights are human rights,' that there was really a revolution in the way women's rights were regarded. At the time, the UN women's rights convention was just being considered. Now it's been ratified by 187 countries.

Those changes to women's rights came about not because of governments, military support or multinational corporations – in fact, all three of those groups tried to stop it – it happened because small groups of determined people harnessed the dream of freedom. That's what's driven women's rights and that's what will continue to drive it. That's why the rise of the NGOs and the rise of women's empowerment is so threatening to the male-dominated world – it's unstoppable.

We've had setbacks. We've had people in increasing power across Europe who don't believe in women's rights. We've had Donald Trump. We have the increasing dominance of Putin, who changed the law in Russia last year to make it legal to beat up your wife – to make domestic violence legal. And we've the creeping dominance of China, which is not known for its progressive women's rights agenda. Nonetheless, I feel very optimistic because I think that the trajectory of women's rights is on the rise and it has been for the last thirty years.

It's definitely getting better. First of all, every time there is exposure of some big societal problem, most people say, 'Oh, my gosh, that's awful. I didn't know about child brides,' or whatever. Every time that happens I'm jumping up and down with glee. Because the only way human rights abuses can persist is under cover of dark, where people don't notice or don't know about it or aren't exposed to it. As soon as something's exposed it's got a

limited lifespan: people are going to stop it. People are going to
rally around it. People are going to start creating change,
putting pressure.

That's what's happening with the women's rights movement.
Who had ever heard of genital mutilation twenty-five years
ago? By the time they graduated from high school my daugh-
ters could tell you fifteen different ways in which women are
abused. So people are starting to create change, to demand
change. That's what the #MeToo movement is about. So I feel
very, very encouraged.

I share Kennedy's optimism for so many reasons. First, a greater
number of countries, multinational organisations and non-gov-
ernment agencies around the world recognise that women's
rights are human rights and are prepared to act in a concerted
effort to promote them. There are fewer places for human
rights violators to hide and it is much easier to bring the world's
attention to violations that are taking place. In my own country,
I see the engagement of young people in discussing complex
issues such as global food insecurity or female genital mutilation, and I believe that the same awakening exists in other
nations, too. There are new tools to send messages all round
the world and new ways to lobby governments to take action.
With electorates that are willing to make demands of what
should be placed high up on a government's agenda, the only
thing that threatens to slow the pace of change is public will.
If there is donor or activist fatigue, or a generation takes for
granted that things will naturally get better without anyone
having to advocate it, there may be a slip. However, if groups

of committed citizens continue to articulate the case for change and demand that it is met, I am more hopeful than ever that world-changing advances are within our grasp.

SANDI TOKSVIG
Broadcaster

Sandi Toksvig is a writer, broadcaster, actor, playwright and comedian. Starting out in children's television, she has appeared across countless UK radio and television comedy shows such as The News Quiz, Who's Line is it Anyway? *and* Call My Bluff. *She currently hosts the BBC's comedy panel show* QI, *is quizmaster on Channel 4's* Fifteen to One *and co-hosts* The Great British Bake Off. *In March 2015, Toksvig co-founded The Women's Equality Party, which now has over 70 branches across the UK and stood candidates in the London, Welsh and Scottish elections of 2016 as well as the 2017 UK General Election. The Women's Equality Party campaigns for equal representation in politics, business and education, equal pay, equal parenting rights and an end to violence against women.*

❝ My father was a foreign correspondent for Danish television so most of my childhood was on the move. My earliest skill – probably at the age of four – was room service. I grew up in hotels.

I grew up in large areas of Africa, in Europe and most particularly in the United States. We were based near the UN; because in those days if you wanted to access as many countries as possible that was the best way for a country with very little money like Denmark to do that.

I grew up with a tremendous sense of the global situation. My father expected us – probably from the age of eight – to read at least the first three pages of the *New York Times* every evening before dinner – in order so that we would have some conversation. And he expected us to have a view.

He didn't mind what the view was. He didn't mind what our political take was, but he minded very much if we didn't have a view.

So I grew up knowing you can make a good life anywhere in the world, that every place has something to commend it and that prejudice comes out of ignorance.

I have a British mother and my father got posted to London when I was sixteen. He went on to become a member of the European Parliament for Denmark but by the time he did that I was already at university here. So I stayed in the UK, really because I was put into the education system here at sixteen. But if I have a hometown, it's New York.

I'm extremely fond of Denmark and still have a house there and my Danish roots are enormously important to me. My father was Danish to his core and Danish food and culture are still enormously important to me. But mostly I'm what I think they call a cultural mongrel.

I always had the sense of wanting to do some good in the world. From early on I wanted to be a human rights lawyer. I wanted to defend people who had suffered injustice. And then I studied law and discovered that really 'the law' isn't what I thought it was. It isn't about justice, it's really about who has got the most money. I was depressed and disillusioned by my study of the law.

I was in Cambridge and was in something called the Footlights – a comedy thing – with Hugh Laurie, Emma Thompson, Stephen Fry and Tony Slattery. That was the gang at the time. And I was seen by a director in a student show and he said, 'Come and work for me for a year in a professional theatre.'

And I thought, Good idea – I'll have a gap year after university as well as before. Fundamentally, I'm having the longest gap year in history. I never went back.

I went into children's television and I liked my work. I enjoyed it. I was good at making telly. My Dad had made telly. I had gone into the family business making telly.

The comedy vein for me is that my whole family is funny. Also, it's the most brilliant defence mechanism. If people are having a go at you because you're 'other', they think you're a bit strange, they won't come near you if they think you're going to make a smart remark about them.

What I love is women's sense of humour – we laugh at very different things.

We had the most glorious moment on the most recent series of *QI* – I was just so happy. We had a marvellous British-Asian woman panellist come on called Sindhu Vee and we were doing a thing where we had coconuts, screwdrivers and hammers.

The boys had to open a coconut and they were just making the most terrible mess of it. And she went, 'This is easy' and just picked up the coconut, stood up and smashed it on the concrete floor of the studio and scooped it up before any of the milk spilled, in two perfect halves.

And it was a wonderful moment of a powerful women doing something incredible that she said every woman in her family knows how to do – there is no way you wouldn't know how to open a coconut – it's just part of her upbringing. But it was just a great moment of the boys being ridiculous with tools and the woman just going – bang, there you go – sorted.

Women bring a different quality. They laugh at different things. That notion that women aren't funny is ridiculous. But it persists and I don't know why it persists. 🙶

FRANCES O'GRADY
General secretary,
Trades Union Congress

The most senior trade unionist in the UK, Frances O'Grady has been active in the movement her entire working life, rising up the ranks at the same time as raising her children as a single mother. She's campaigned for the national minimum wage, equal pay for women, and workers' rights. In January 2013, she became the general secretary of the TUC, the first woman to hold this post in its 150-year history.

❝ This wasn't something I had planned, beyond the fact that I always wanted to contribute to the trade-union movement. I'm a trade unionist, not a politician – that's my thing. I know the politics is important but I love stuff about work – I'm nosy about work. When I was organising, I liked to go around the back and find out what was going on and talking to workers.

I had been active in the Transport and General Workers Union. I loved it and my family was active as well, so it was a normal thing. I applied for a job at the T&G after I had had Hannah, my daughter. And when I became a single parent I applied for a job at the TUC (because it was closer – don't tell anybody!).

I came to the TUC as a campaigns officer. It was certainly not my plan or ambition to end up as general secretary. But I did a number of different jobs, like setting up the organising academy to train young organisers, mostly women, and felt very strongly that the trade-union movement needed to change. I wanted to see more women at every level and the movement looking more like the workforce we wanted to organise. I became head of organisation when I was relatively young for the TUC, and was quite nervous. We had regional secretaries – whom some described as the barons – blokes in their fifties, and I was in my thirties, being their boss. In fact, they were incredibly encouraging and supportive.

It's a cliché, but it can be lonely at the top. Who can you talk to when you're really pissed off? You have to put a smile on your face, though, because you need to bring people together. And you might be dealing with a group of really macho men who think banging the table is the way to your heart. It took a bit of education for some to grasp that that didn't impress me and it wasn't the style that was going to work with me. But I also believe it's the best job in the world – it's a job that makes a difference to people.

Sometimes you feel like you've been put in somebody else's world and haven't been given the rule book: you don't know what's expected or how to behave or what you should be going for. In the trade-union movement there were times when I used to wonder, Where's the bible that explains exactly what's going on? It took me ages to realise I could write a new one: I didn't have to following somebody else's. **"**

10

Looking Back and Paying It Forward

The Danish philosopher Søren Kierkegaard said, 'Life can only be understood backwards, but it must be lived forwards.' It's the sort of statement that can be made so emphatically only with the benefit of years.

When you are young, every possibility still exists – at eight, I *could* still have gone on to win Wimbledon – but every decision made, path chosen and year concluded narrows your field of vision. I will now never be a famous sportsperson or go on a Club 18–30 holiday or be able to do a backflip. I will never marry Joey from New Kids on the Block, or become the sheriff, snooker player or archaeologist of my childhood dreams.

Equally, for all the things I thought I *could* be when I grew up, there was no indication to me of what I *would* be. Maybe editing my primary-school yearbook pointed to journalism, or high-school debating competitions indicated some form of public speaking. But even if I'd considered politics – which simply wasn't on my radar – no such thing as a Scottish parliament existed back then, so leading the Scottish Conservatives was so far beyond my ken, it was utterly foreign.

I wonder if I would be a disappointment to my younger self. I certainly think I would be a surprise.

When I was in high school, one of the biggest shows on television was *Absolutely Fabulous*. The absurdist comedy was based on the premise of two ageing fashionistas acting like teenagers, while the teenage daughter of one – Saffy – acted like a grown-up. One day I was called into the head of career guidance's office to be told that a journalist had phoned the school. She was doing an article for a Sunday magazine on 'The Saffy Syndrome' and interviewing half a dozen sensible teenagers from schools across the UK. 'You've always got a lot to say for yourself, Ruth. Will you talk to her?'

That weekend, I took a call from a journalist based in London (which seemed hopelessly exotic) on the BT Bakelite rotary dial phone in my parents' kitchen in my wee village in Fife. The journalist pressed me for my hopes and ambitions, my world view, politics and pastimes. She then sent a photographer north to take a picture of me in my school uniform, inexplicably holding a ghetto-blaster on my shoulder. I still have the magazine.

It seems that – along with my desire to go to university, get a good job and my belief that early Margaret Thatcher was better than late Thatcher and the Iron Lady should have called it a day sooner – I was most keen to be married by twenty-three and have two children by about thirty. Clearly, it had not occurred to me that I could be writing a book discussing my teenage self as an unmarried, pregnant gay woman of thirty-nine. At least I never considered becoming a futurologist or clairvoyant.

While I have made a thousand mistakes – not least the loose perm I once insisted upon, which made my head look like a dark brown cauliflower – I'm not sure how much of my growing up I would actually change. Every decision taken has led me to where I am now. And where I am sees me more comfortable in my own skin than I have been at any point probably since puberty. I wouldn't give up any of the relationships I've had – even the ones that have been hurtful or ended badly. I wouldn't swap any of the employers I've worked for or the countries I've visited or the scrapes I've got myself into. Every single one is part of the road that has led me here.

What I would like to do is go back and reassure my younger self that it will all work out in the end. All the broken bones, tearful goodbyes or exciting new dawns are nothing to be afraid of. I wouldn't want the decisions necessarily to change, but I'd like greater emotional confidence as I made them.

I'd like to tell my teenage self not to be intimidated by posh blowhards, to accept my own sexuality sooner and in a far more forgiving way. To realise being funny doesn't necessarily make you unladylike, and it's okay to prefer vodka and Diet Coke to Cabernet Sauvignon.

I *might* urge myself not to give up alcohol for Lent in 1998 – it led me to start smoking, so that I had something to do with my hands while everyone else was drinking pints. It took me three years to give up again. And I would love to tell the younger me not to spend so many years without the greatest joy you can have in a house, other than people: a dog. But, other than those two, I'm not sure I'd advise anything different on decision-making.

I was interested in my subjects – what could a self-made dot-com millionaire possibly want to change about their life? Or the prime minister of a G7 nation? Or a five-times Olympic medallist? Well, it turns out we've all learned things along the way that we wish our younger selves had known.

Similarly, we are all products of our time, and times change. Every generation stands on the shoulders of the one that went before, choosing either to repeat their mistakes or learn from them.

I am acutely aware of how much I owe to the generations that have gone before. Not just the women who marched to get the vote – those who chained themselves to railings and were subject to the Cat and Mouse Act, which meant force-feeding during hunger strikes in prison – but also those for whom the very fact of quietly getting things done in their own lives and own sphere pushed the boundaries: the women who went to work during the First World War, changing the opportunities and acceptance of women in the workplace; those who cast off skirts in favour of trousers, changing perceptions of women from the merely decorative to the thoroughly practical.

Then there were the women who refused to believe that their employment had to stop as soon as their boyfriend became their husband, and who changed employment culture and practice, and the women who came back to work after having children – and those who demanded time off before doing so – changing how maternity provision was enshrined in law.

And there were the women who entered Parliament, or film,

or the sporting world, those women who put their heads above the parapet and themselves firmly in the public eye, enduring the taunts, mockery and misogyny that came their way, and did it anyway. They cleared a path for those who followed.

And let's not forget the women who taught in schools, opening minds and expanding horizons, those women who looked at the eager faces in front of them and told them that just because something hadn't yet been done didn't mean it shouldn't be.

And there were all those women who went first – whatever their particular first was – and made it easier for those who came after. Just as technological change is speeding up, it can seem that advancement is slowing down. The high peaks – the right to vote, to work, to property, to equal pay – have all been scaled in law. Yet we still see a gender gap in recruitment advancement and remuneration in practice. Perhaps cultural shifts are a harder summit than legislative change.

There's the practical side, too. When the world is open before you and every possibility exists, how do you decide which of the many paths to follow – and what happens if you want to change path?

I remember distinctly the exquisite, hopeful, despairing, joyful, tortuous, clear-sighted confusion of being fifteen. I had aced my first set of exams and was two years away from the two greatest freedoms I could possibly conceive: driving and moving out of home to go to university. I had bought a second-hand electric guitar – that I would never learn to play – from a boy I wanted to impress and hung around one of the school bands that played Guns N' Roses covers, doing lighting or a bit of backing dancing when required. I wrote dodgy poetry, played sport competently and was sold alcohol at the local off-licence on a Friday night but still got into the football half-price on a child's ticket on a Saturday afternoon.

I already knew more than my parents, and any anxieties I had – over my body, my relationships or my future – were for the dark times, not the daylight hours. If I magically transported myself back to the nineties, I'm not sure that my fifteen-year-old self would listen to a word I had to say. Just as I'm not sure that fifteen-year-olds now would think someone who grew up without a mobile phone or the internet, who didn't have a shower in the house until they were ten, and were in their twenties before they had access to more than five TV channels, could possibly have any wisdom to pass on.

But it's part of being human to want to make things easier. To use your own failings and failures, fears and frustrations to guide those who come after, whether they want to take that guidance or not. So here is what these amazing, ceiling-shattering, world-changing women would tell their younger selves, and how they would encourage girls on the cusp of womanhood now.

Martha Lane Fox

If I could tell myself something that I wish I had known, I'd say that there's never any downside to being as generous-spirited as possible. I don't say that because I have been horrible or mean the whole way through my life, but I feel that I have wasted time worrying about including people, or not including people, or positioning in a particular way. To fifteen-year-olds now I would say that if you can become fearless in using technology and understanding it, you will always be employable. It's astonishing how many jobs are available in the technology sector, and I am concerned that we have gone back to the situation that existed twenty-five to thirty years ago when there are so few women in the sector. We need you. Be ambitious.

Rola Hallam

The thing that has allowed me not just to survive but thrive was making friends with uncertainty. I would tell myself, 'You're going to make a lot of plans and then they're going to change very dramatically,' because there's what you plan, and then there's reality and what actually happens. So be flexible, be adaptable and embrace uncertainty: if you try to go always for what is certain you'll have a miserable life and probably achieve very little.

To others, my message is, You can do it. *You can do it.* You are only limited by your perception of your potential. If you say, 'This is what I can do,' that is all you will ever do. And if you say, 'The sky's the limit,' I believe it is. You can do it.

Frances O'Grady

I think I'd tell myself that it'll all be all right. I think I did all right, in the sense that I always worked from a young age. I always had jobs and I learned a lot from that. I probably worked too many hours but I had a sense of independence that stood me in good stead.

For others? Go for what makes you happy, what you feel passionate about, because if you find that, you'll do well in it.

Also, find somebody who's senior to you, a woman who's senior to you, who will support and encourage you. But find a woman who's starting out even younger than you were and support her – it's that sense of women standing on each other's shoulders. The final thing I would say is, it's never too late. I see loads and loads of women in their fifties who finally feel, 'This is me-time,' and I would say, 'Go for it.'

Laura Kuenssberg

I would tell myself that I could do it. I used to think that it would be absolutely astonishing if I ever got to be what I wanted to be. I had a very loving upbringing and was brought up to think, Yeah, you can work hard and do everything, but the idea of editing the ten o'clock news or doing this kind of job felt unattainable. I think that if I had been less worried, I might have taken more risks.

To fifteen-year-olds now? Work really hard and be really nice. That sounds corny, but work harder than everybody else. Ask the stupid question because people will try to ask the really clever question and it's nearly always the stupid question that prompts the answer you really want.

Lorna Hood

Stick with it and it'll work out. Stick with it and you're not on your own. I think that's the main thing. You're not on your own. There's always help and support.

Be careful. Cover your drink. Watch out for social media. Respect yourself, and respect the gifts and talents you have.

Believe that you can do anything and go anywhere. You can get to the top in anything in life if you're willing to use the gifts and talents that you've got and just be yourself. Don't try to be anybody else. Be yourself and it'll work. Keep smiling.

Maria Bello

You've just got to laugh at yourself, at your circumstances, at the world.

After I have a big cry sometimes, when something totally disastrous or painful has happened in my life, eventually I get to the place where I laugh and I realise life goes on and always gets better.

I say to today's young people, 'Travel, travel, travel, see the world.' It's about getting outside your community and seeing different people's experiences.

Melinda Gates

You're stronger than you know. Lean in. So, whatever it is you're uncomfortable about as a woman, or whatever you're trying to do, lean into it and have the courage to take that difficult step. You'll be amazed at what you can do.

Don't be afraid, don't be afraid of anything. Be bold.

Tina Brown

To my younger self I'd say, 'Patience, patience, patience' – I'm very impatient. And look before you leap because I've always just rushed into things – which works a lot of the time, but sometimes it doesn't.

To today's fifteen-year-olds: log off. Social media is a confidence destroyer. The fear of missing out on stuff is a killer. You're not missing out. You can stay at home with a book. You can stay at home and have your own quiet space. Do not think that you have to be participating in this constant competitive social jamboree of these photographs of everybody with a beer. Being a popular person can sometimes mean being a hollow person. There's nothing wrong with your own company. Solitude and some reflection. It just doesn't happen enough.

Seema Rao

Keep an open mind. If you're open, you'll see a lot more of what life can offer you than if you have a one-track mind.

Theresa May

My advice to my younger self would be to have more confidence in myself. I'm a great believer that it's important for women, whatever they're involved in, whether it's politics or business, that they believe in themselves and believe in how they're doing things. Don't feel you've got to fit a stereotype.

My message to fifteen-year-olds today is, don't feel your options are limited by the fact that you're a girl. Know the world is your oyster. Believe in yourself.

Sheila Marcelo

Be authentically bold. That's a hard one to tell a fifteen-year-old. Authenticity requires a sense of vulnerability and comfort in your insecurity and imperfection. It's tough to talk to a fifteen-year-old about that, but what's so interesting about that vulnerability is it's inherently your strength and it is what makes you more human and stronger. And then the bold part: it's taking risks, and taking risks to the point that it's okay to be judged, it's okay to fail. When you're fifteen those things are tough.

Going through the pitfalls of life is what makes it rich. It makes us embrace who we end up becoming. Life has a lot of turns and things evolve. Make sure you're living in the moment, taking deep breaths. Be your authentic self.

Ruth Ibegbuna

I'd tell myself to stop caring so much about what other people think of my ability and me, and to allow myself to fly. I think I was a very bright girl and, like a lot of girls in state school, I'd try to hide it because it's not cool. I wished I'd embraced it more, been more vigorous with it and pushed myself even harder.

To others I'd say be focused and be fierce. Just those two things.

Katherine Grainger

It's easy at fifteen to compare yourself with others and think that if your ambitions are different from everyone else's then you're wrong, or alone or unusual. Confidence is massive, so believe in yourself and believe what you believe.

Everyone at that age assumes everyone else is okay and they're not. And it's about reassurance that everyone is still finding the path and what is right for them. That struggle is right and normal, and it's good that you don't know. Don't follow the path just because it's there. Make your own path.

Gemma Fay

Change is good. Find a way to love yourself. That's the most important thing.

Sue Black

I would tell my younger self, 'Don't go against what you know in your heart is right,' because you rarely make a mistake if you know something's right for you. If you listen to other people, they'll change your mind, but they have a different agenda. You know what fits for you. What fits you at fifteen may not fit you at twenty-one, but at fifteen you've still got to go with what fits you and that, I think, helps to give you a solid identity. You're going to make mistakes, of course you'll make mistakes, but listen to your heart more than to your head and more than you listen to the people around you. If it's right for you, go for it!

The advice I have for today's fifteen-year-olds is that there is nothing you can't do in this world now – absolutely nothing. There are things your mother couldn't do, things your grand-mother couldn't do. There are things your great-grandmother couldn't do, because the world was the way it was. Right now, there is nothing that you cannot do as a girl.

Acknowledgements

My thanks to each and every one of the women who allowed me to interview them for this book, and to all women who have made a new first, who've moved the dial or have tried to make it easier for those who come after.

My thanks, too, to Daniel Guild for his amazing powers of research and logistical planning; and to Ann Menzies for her patience in transcribing hours of recorded conversation into usable text.

And, of course, to my partner Jen. Turns out I'm a pain in the arse when I'm writing a book. Thanks for putting up with me, pet. I'll tidy up my papers tomorrow . . .

Index

An invitation from the publisher

Join us at www.hodder.co.uk, or follow us
on Twitter @hodderbooks to be a part of
our community of people who love the very
best in books and reading.

Whether you want to discover more about a book
or an author, watch trailers and interviews, have the
chance to win early limited editions, or simply browse
our expert readers' selection of the very best books,
we think you'll find what you're looking for.

And if you don't, that's the place to tell us what's missing.

We love what we do, and we'd love you to be a part of it.

www.hodder.co.uk

 @hodderbooks

 HodderBooks

 HodderBooks